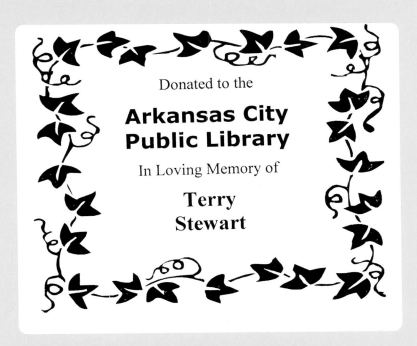

Training Your Pointing Dog
for Hunting and Home

Training Your Pointing Dog for Hunting and Home

RICHARD D. WEAVER

STACKPOLE BOOKS

Published by
STACKPOLE BOOKS
5067 Ritter Road
Mechanicsburg, PA 17055
www.stackpolebooks.com

Printed in China

First edition

10 9 8 7 6 5 4 3 2 1

Photographs by author except where otherwise noted

Library of Congress Cataloging-in-Publication Data

Weaver, Richard (Richard D.)
  Training your pointing dog for hunting and home / Richard Weaver. — 1st ed.
      p. cm.
  Includes index.
  ISBN-13: 978-0-8117-0259-1
  ISBN-10: 0-8117-0259-6
  1. Pointing dogs—Training. I. Title.

SF428.5.W374 2007
636.752'535—dc22

                                                        2006037446

CONTENTS

DEDICATION

To all puppies, past, present, and future—may they always give me a sense of renewal.

Dark Hollow Tuck with son Dark Hollow Spiller at four months.

INTRODUCTION

The training process and additional information in the pages that follow are the product of thirty-five years of experience and a thousand-plus dogs. My intention is to provide the reader with a simplified, commonsense approach to training the companion pointing dog. You can use the process in its entirety or to troubleshoot individual aspects of your dog's education. It is uncomplicated, and can work equally well for the novice or experienced handler. The goal is to develop your dog's natural aptitudes to the fullest possible extent on your own or with the aid of a professional at critical moments. Companion gun dogs are best raised and trained by their owners as much as possible, though when necessary, you can seek help from a competent pro who specializes in companion gun dogs.

Some of what you read in these pages may differ from the procedures outlined elsewhere by competitive trainers in field trials or the show ring. The needs and goals of the typical companion gun dog and its owner-handler are quite different from those of field-trial or show prospects. They are not lesser or greater, just different. Be aware of this throughout the process of choosing, raising, and training your dog.

Puppies generally are not born with behavior problems; a problem dog is likely the result of improper handling and training. Most problems stem from a lack of control that manifests itself in the field, where the level of distraction is the greatest. The answer lies in effective, early obedience training, positive reinforcement, and proper transition to the field. Not all pups have the potential to be superdogs, but most can be reasonably proficient field companions and loyal friends.

Excuses for poorly trained dogs vary from not having the time to not having the knowledge to train a gun dog. But most people should be

Tuck at six years with AyA and grouse.

capable of reading and understanding a training book, and if you really have the motivation, you can allot fifteen minutes a day to training. If you cannot or will not make this commitment, don't invest in a pup that will go untrained and unattended. Since you are putting time, money, and emotion into this project, give yourself a chance to succeed by starting with the right breed for your temperament and type of hunting. If you're not sure what kind of dog is right for you, contact a knowledgeable, unbiased professional or refer to a book that covers the strengths and weaknesses of all breeds.

Because you have purchased a training manual for the pointing breeds, you likely have already chosen a pointing-dog pup from proven bloodlines for your type of use (although chapter 2 can help you find a competent breeder, if you have not yet done so). The training schedule provided in this book is organized according to age categories and the lessons to be learned during each. The schedule may vary in timing, depending on your pup's temperament and maturation. If your pup is precocious, you may get ahead of schedule. If it is timid, you may fall behind. Adjust your pace to suit you and your dog, and move on to the next step only when you think your dog is ready.

When training a dog that does not have to meet specific show or trial standards, your approach can be more flexible. If you wish to use different terminology, that's fine. It's important to be confident and comfortable with the words and techniques you use. Your confidence will transfer to your dog and serve you well during training and hunting. Always act as if you know what you're doing. Your dog's response will be based more on your demeanor than on your words.

If you use the techniques and timing in the text correctly, the result will be a companion gun dog you will be proud to own. I dislike shortcuts and do not use gimmicks as a substitute for solid training, time, and patience. Given good bloodlines and good training, you won't need extreme methods, and few problems will develop. Good luck and get to it!

CHAPTER ONE

Planning Training Sessions

Now that you've accepted the responsibility of training your own dog, you should incorporate two rules into your training: be consistent and be persistent in your approach. If you observe these two rules, you will be more likely to succeed.

CONSISTENCY

Always use the same word, hand or whistle signal, or lead pressure for the lesson being taught. For example, if "come" is the signal to bring your dog to you, always use it. Do not say "come on," "come here," "here," or some other term. Train yourself to be a consistent handler, and your pup will become a better-trained adult. Also, never give a command you cannot enforce. This is the cardinal rule of dog training. Picking words and signals that are more natural and comfortable to you will help. Do not send mixed messages, which will confuse the dog and frustrate you.

Stay on an even emotional level, remaining firm but reassuring. Pups that are either coddled or overly berated will not respond well. If you approach training in a calm, confident manner, the pup will develop into a calm, confident adult.

PERSISTENCE

Never allow a pup to disobey a command and then expect it to listen the next time. It won't. You command and the dog obeys, always.

For best results, take your puppy from its mother and littermates at around seven weeks of age (subject to dog laws in your state). Scientific evidence suggests that this is the optimum time in the pup's development to do so. Its capacity to learn is as great at seven weeks as it will ever be, even though emotional development is just beginning. Doing this will allow you to best take advantage of your pup's natural instincts to shape its personality in a manner that suits it to living in a human social pack. In effect, you will become the leader of the pack, and your pup will naturally

Dark Hollow Corey play sight-pointing at ten weeks.

look to you for leadership. Using a fail-safe, positively reinforced approach can prevent behavior problems.

Actual training sessions should begin as soon as the puppy is secure in its new environment and is beginning to trust you—at around nine to ten weeks of age, or about two weeks after you brought the pup home. When the pup is very young, sessions should be no longer than fifteen minutes and take place twice a day, or at least once a day, depending on your schedule. Spend additional time just playing with the pup, taking it for walks and expanding its environment. A pup's attention tends to wander like a small child's. If your puppy shows signs of tiring, repeat a command you know it will complete successfully, praise the pup, and then quit. Training sessions should be something the puppy looks forward to each day. Keep them positive.

Don't try to cram too much into one training session, one day, or one week. Accomplish one or two simple commands at a time, then move on to other, more difficult ones. At first these training sessions should be between you and your pup alone, with no distractions. Once you have instilled good obedience and the pup has developed sufficient maturity, you can gradually introduce distractions.

Do not lose your temper, and do not discipline during training sessions. Be firm but patient. Show the pup what you want it to do, use proper technique to enforce your command, and praise the animal when it gets it right. If a young pup fails during early yard training, it is the handler's fault. My technique involves a tried-and-true, positive-reinforcement approach to training, using reassuring firmness when handling the pup. This approach ensures success, builds confidence in the pup, and encourages it to look forward to the next session.

At first keep the pup always on a lead to control it and to guarantee success with each and every command. Praise appropriately when the pup does well, but don't overdo it. At this stage in the pup's life, praise and positive reinforcement are the law. Later, when the youngster knows what to do but refuses, you will introduce negative sanctions into your training regimen. Go from a short to a progressively longer lead, using it to ensure success and show the pup you are in control at any distance. The pup should eventually think you are omnipresent. If you plan to use an electronic collar, you should not introduce it until the pup has first

German shorthair pup sight-pointing at seven weeks. DONNIE EBERSOLE

learned its commands, employing it only for reinforcement of commands and problem solving.

As Joel Vance of *Gun Dog* magazine once wrote, "Simple is best, and firmness beats hysteria." Above all, be patient! There is no shortcut to a well-trained, well-adjusted dog.

CANINE PSYCHOLOGY

Many new owners never give their pup's thought process much consideration and simply try to impose their will upon the dog. Others fall prey to popular myths that attempt to use human psychology to explain canine behavior. Dogs' brains are not wired the same way human brains are. Yes, they are social animals, and properly interpreted, that fact can be used to the owner's benefit. However, we must first understand that at the heart of canine behavior is the tendency to dominate or be dominated. This is not as harsh as it may sound. To physically dominate is to possess the ability to lead the pack. In the wild, the contest for physical domination would be ongoing. Through appropriate interpretation and response to a pup's behavior, we can eliminate that daily struggle and in a natural fashion, make ourselves dominant for the duration of our relationship with our canine companion.

This does not mean mistreating your dog! To the contrary, regular obedience training and techniques such as the alpha roll can go a long way to accomplishing this goal. The alpha roll is not used during training sessions. When your youngster is being openly defiant, resisting handling, growling, or trying to exert its dominance in some other manner, simply pin it to the ground with one hand on the side of its neck and the other hand on its side around the loin. At first the pup will fight and resist, but it will eventually go limp. More dominant pups will take longer to submit. After the pup submits, let it get up and resume normal activity. You have simply shown the pup your ability to physically dominate it. Along with regular obedience sessions, this exercise will establish you as the leader in the relationship.

Your pup needs to understand that you are in charge of making the decisions. For example, a pup does not decide whether or not to jump; you do. A pup does not decide whether to chew furniture or move so you can enter a doorway it is blocking; you do. One of the most common problematic myths is that dogs do things to please us or to displease us. No they don't; they are not wired that way. Dogs do things to please themselves, and because they can. If it feels good, they want to do it; if not, they avoid it. At the base of all training, we must make the behavior we find undesirable uncomfortable enough so that the dog does not want to do it. Likewise, behavior we want to instill needs to be rewarded to make it sufficiently pleasing to the dog. Once the lesson is learned, Rover will sit—not to please you, but rather to receive the reward that makes the behavior pleasing to him.

When Rover wags his tail, jumps on you and licks your face, it is not because he loves you. Instead, it shows that the pup does not respect your authority. And if the pup does not respect your authority, you can forget about controlling it in the field. Being too lenient or too harsh results in failure because the pup will not trust or respect its owner. The amount of positive or negative reinforcement to use depends on the breed and the individual dog. What may deter one dog from chasing deer may be simply ignored by another. This is where learning to read your dog is critical. Too much correction may cower a dog and too little may create a misbehaved monster.

Rose with limit of Pennsylvania grouse at three years.

I often use the phrase "reassuring firmness" when teaching owners how to approach their dog. Find the appropriate level of firmness for your dog, and then maintain this level when handling the dog. Do not fluctuate from coddling to expressing anger or frustration. Stay emotionally even so that your pup will trust you, know what to expect from you, and respond to your handling.

Even more significant is that a properly trained dog that knows its place and clearly understands the parameters of acceptable behavior will be a happier, more self-assured individual. This is simply because the dog is not always butting heads with its human companions and being disciplined for doing so. Instead, the dog will take the path of least resistance; in other words, the dog will do what brings it pleasure. Ultimately, understanding how your dog thinks and responds to stimuli will help you shape it into a good citizen around the house and a competent performer in the field. ∎

CHAPTER TWO

The First Seven Weeks

If you are not breeding and raising your own litter, the first seven weeks of your pup's life will not be under your direct supervision. Still, you may use the information in this chapter to determine how well the breeder socializes pups, and if you reserve a pup before the litter is born, you may ask the breeder to perform these tasks to ensure the pup's proper development. Be sure he or she is breeding proven bloodlines for the use you plan for your dog. If possible, visit the breeder, check the facilities, and get a demonstration in the field with one or both parents. Picking the litter is the most critical task. When picking an individual from a quality litter, stay away from extremes in size and temperament. Such pups are more likely to have health or behavior problems.

This chapter is intended to help you better socialize your pup. Like human babies, it is important for puppies to form meaningful attachments early in their lives. Their mother is the first such attachment. The person who helps whelp the pups and is around them in the first days and weeks of their lives will be the second. When you first get your pup, it will be somewhat upset by the changes in its life. The more time you spend with it and the more attention you give it, the sooner it will bond with you. Pups need to be exposed to humans and other dogs, as well as a variety of situations, to develop stable, outgoing personalities. Well-socialized pups will make the adjustment to a new home more easily and take training more readily.

The following schedule for socializing pups during their first seven weeks reflects my own approach but also was influenced by George Bird Evan's *Troubles with Bird Dogs*, Richard Wolter's *Gun Dog*, and canine behavioral research done at Massachusetts Institute of Technology.

A mother's nurture is the most critical element during the first week of a pup's life.

THE FIRST FOUR WEEKS
Introduce Human Stimuli
Begin during the pups' first moments of life. If necessary you may assist in the delivery. Help stimulate the newborn pups by rubbing them gently with a clean towel and inspecting them for abnormalities. Puppies and mother will become accustomed to your being part of the rearing process, and the puppies will get an early start in responding to human stimuli.

Introduce Mild Stress
Pick up the pups, roll them over and stroke them, and hold them vertically head-up and head-down at least once daily. If possible, members of both sexes should handle the pups this way. Do not overly stress the pups or keep them away from their mother for too long. This exercise is particularly important during weeks three and four.

Introduce Noise
Make various sounds and vibrations, proceeding only as the pups' reactions show they are ready. At no time should you overly alarm the pups. If they are being raised inside, the television or radio can help with this process. Never introduce gunfire at this time; you are many training steps and months away from this all-important step in a gun dog's development.

Start Self-Feeding and Weaning
At the end of the third week, you can start the weaning process by teaching the puppies to lap from a dish. Most pups will take to lapping quite naturally, although an occasional puppy may need your help and encouragement. Hold each pup, showing it the dish but being careful not to submerge its nose. Water is a good starter for lapping. You can use a mixture of dry baby cereal, dry milk, and warm water to start feeding. Use this mixture for only a few days, increasing its thickness each feeding. Next, puree a mixture of dry puppy food, canned food, and warm water. Again, start with a liquefied mixture and gradually increase the thickness.

WEEKS FOUR AND FIVE
Continue Supplemental Feeding and Begin Weaning
Continue feeding the mixture of dry puppy food, canned food, and warm water through weeks four and five. By five weeks, a good soaking and

spoon mixing should be enough. Increase the amount of food and number of feedings while gradually taking the mother away.

Start Teaching Names

If names have been chosen, you can start teaching them at this time by using them each time you handle each pup. Again, the breeder should be willing to do this for you, if you have selected your pup by this age. Soon the pups will begin to recognize and respond to their names.

Continue Loud Noises

Hand clapping and pan rattling will help accustom the pups to loud noises. Take care not to frighten the pups, and do not shoot over them yet. Proceed as the pups' temperaments and responses allow.

Six-week-old English setter pups—content and waiting to go to new homes.

Pups are well socialized and ready to go to new homes at seven weeks.

Start Teaching the Pup to Come

When feeding, set the food dishes down at a distance, and call or whistle for the pups to come, using the food as an enticement. You can also start to kneel and use excited gestures while calling "come," or using the whistle. Pups must eventually learn to come to both the verbal and whistle signals. At this age, the pup will respond more to your body language, but it will soon learn come by association. Always praise when a pup comes to you. This remains a rule throughout training.

WEEKS SIX AND SEVEN

Continue Feeding

Each litter is unique, but usually by six weeks of age, the puppies should be completely weaned and receiving three feedings a day. By this age, the pups should be eating dry puppy food right from the bag.

Continue to Socialize

At this age, socialization becomes even more important. Contacts with pups should be frequent and involve different people and environments. Children can be good for pups, if properly supervised and old enough to display judgment.

Also, continue loud noises, but still no gunfire!

Start Car Rides

Keep these short at first, and try to do something enjoyable at the end of the ride. Increase the distance gradually as the pup's reaction allows. It may be necessary to start by just sitting with the motor idling, then proceed to short rides.

Continue to Teach the Pup to Come

At this point, use the kneeling position, excited gestures, and an encouraging voice tone to get the puppy to come to you. Associate the verbal and whistle command, and praise the pup when it comes.

BRINGING YOUR PUPPY HOME

At seven weeks (forty-nine days), the puppy should be taken from the litter to its new home. If the lessons above have not been started, you need to teach them yourself. If your pup is well enough socialized, separation anxiety will be minimal.

Upon bringing your pup to its new home, your first job is to develop good dog-master rapport. Dogs are pack animals and thus look for leadership instinctively. You must become the leader of the pack, or the alpha dog. Your pup must trust you and your leadership. When you have properly created this early bond through caring and positive reinforcement, you will have taken a giant step toward developing your future companion gun dog.

For the next week or two, continue to teach the pup its name by using it every time you touch or talk to the animal. Also continue to teach "come" with the same kneeling, hand gesture, and voice tone approach. Do not encourage disobedience by using "come" when the pup is overly distracted and obviously not going to listen. Choose your moments, and otherwise go pick the puppy up.

Finally, you must begin to housebreak your pup. You and your pup's future will be more pleasant if the pup is crate-broken, house-broken, and kennel worthy. Hunting trips, visits to family or friends, illness, and other events in your dog's future may require any one of these living accommodations. A pup that is introduced to all of them early will respond better to any of them throughout life. I am a strong proponent of keeping your gun dog in the house with you and your family, but my dogs spend time in all of these environments.

CHAPTER THREE

Puppy Obedience Work

Once your pup has become secure in its new environment and has begun to develop a bond with you and your family, about nine to ten weeks of age, you should begin obedience sessions in an isolated environment, away from distractions. Organize these sessions as described in chapter 1, and wait no longer! You have already made a commitment to your pup for life, so there is no reason to wait. Show and field-trial professionals use a different time schedule and techniques, because their goals demand it. They generally wait until later so that they can evaluate the pups and not waste time on ones they think cannot win. Your goal is to develop your pup into a competent companion gun dog, given whatever natural potential it may possess. You will teach some commands in formal yard sessions and others during the daily routine of living with your pup.

CRATE- AND HOUSEBREAKING

Many owners struggle and never completely succeed with housebreaking, a relatively simple task when done correctly. Do not make it unpleasant for both the pup and yourself. All you are doing is taking advantage of your pup's natural inclination to go outside its den to relieve itself. When properly done, housebreaking is a matter of positive reinforcement of your pup's natural instincts.

When you are at home and can observe the pup full-time, simply keep it under constant observation. When its behavior indicates a need to relieve itself, take the pup outside using the word "out," praise it when finished, and immediately bring it back inside. Using the word "out" each time you go to the door will by association teach the pup to go to the door when it needs to relieve itself. If the pup makes a mistake and you observe the behavior, use "no," then take the pup out as previously described.

Early handling on the grooming table from seven weeks on helps desensitize the pup and make it bolder.

Also establish regular times to take the pup out at logical moments in its daily routine—after strenuous play, a long nap, drinking, or eating.

When you cannot observe the pup, the most humane and effective approach is to confine it to a crate just large enough that it can lie down, stand, and stretch. The pup will naturally not want to soil its own den, just like in the wild. If the crate is too large, the pup will be more likely to go to one end, do its business, and then go back to the other end to curl up and sleep. If you purchase a crate large enough to still fit the pup when it becomes an adult, you can partition one end to the correct size. The crate will also protect your house from damage and the pup from harm, such as chewing on an electric cord. The crate will eventually become the pup's safe haven, and it will go to the crate on command or on its own. Dogs are den animals and naturally seek small, confined places in which to feel secure. Crate-breaking will also help protect your dog from harm when traveling in your vehicle, and if the dog is ever sick or injured, the crate will provide a safe haven.

Do not expect a young pup to hold it in for very long; its muscle control is not yet established, much like a small child. When letting the pup out of the crate, take it immediately to the door, command "out," and follow the same procedure as usual. For a week or two, you may have to get up in the middle of the night. I like to keep the pup's crate in the bedroom at night so I can hear it getting restless and asking to go out. If you have other dogs sleeping in the bedroom, the pup will soon learn proper behavior from their example.

With a little extra time and vigilance, the task of housebreaking can be accomplished in a couple of weeks. With a less intense approach, the job can drag on indefinitely. Once the pup is crate-broken, you can gradually grant more freedom being careful not to allow backsliding.

WEEKS EIGHT TO TWELVE
Throughout these early months, it is also important to expand on your pup's earlier daily living lessons. Continue car rides, gradually lengthening them and having an enjoyable experience for the pup at the destination. Introduce the pup to new environments, anything you want it to accept later in life. Always introduce new experiences in a positive, reassuring fashion, taking caution to guard against overly alarming the pup.

The "no" command should be used for every infraction of the rules from the beginning. A stern voice, accompanied by a firm but gentle shake by the loose skin of the neck, should be sufficient for most pups to quickly learn the meaning. Use only as much firmness as needed to get the job done; let your pup's reaction be your guide. Never strike a pup with your hand or a heavy object; you are not out to harm the pup, only to teach it boundaries for acceptable and unacceptable behavior. This command should become so engrained that your adult companion will respond to it immediately and absolutely. The "no" command is an excellent illustration of the philosophy "Simple is best, and firmness beats hysteria." Do not punish out of anger. Remain in control and under control. You do not want your pup to fear you. As soon as you have given the punishment, pick up your pup and reassure it. Just like a child, your pup should understand that punishment is for certain behaviors, not because you are angry at it. Your pup must learn to trust you and your judgment.

This is the time to start formal yard training. Regular obedience training teaches your pup certain vital commands, but more important, it teaches the pup to look to you for direction, respect you as the alpha animal, and form good behaviors so that you will not need to break bad ones later. When you have achieved proper control, you will have become omnipresent in your pup's mind.

Throughout yard training, it is important to be positive and reassuring. Do not punish during training sessions. Give a command, physically show the pup the correct response, then praise. If there is a breakdown, it is your fault, not the dog's, at this point in time. If pup is having a bad day and you are losing patience, end the session with a simple command the pup will respond to, praise, and quit. When sessions are carefully planned ahead of time, there should be little room for error, and failure will be the exception. Your job is to guide the pup in the proper direction, then praise when it succeeds. This positive approach will build a confident dog and a trusting relationship with you. Once the pup knows what is expected of it and is a little older, you will introduce distractions and use negative reinforcement when necessary.

Condition the Pup to Collar and Leash
Getting the pup used to a collar can be accomplished by simply allowing it to wear the collar when you take it into the yard, on car rides, or for a

romp. Your pup should always have on a collar with identification when it is not in the house or kennel. It is probably best not to leave a collar on a young pup when it is not being supervised. *Never* use a choke chain for anything but training, and not at all until pup is somewhat older. Some soft dogs will never need one.

During training sessions, your pup should always have on both a collar and a lead. To ensure success, you need to always be in position to enforce your commands. You can begin with a six-foot lead and progress to a twenty-five-foot one as needed. Once the pup starts to learn elementary commands up close, the longer check cord allows you to get farther away but remain in control. The pup will sense freedom, but you can show it you are still in charge. The longer lead also facilitates teaching quartering, retrieving, "come," and so on. Sometimes allowing your puppy to just drag the lead around the yard can help accustom the pup to it before you use it for training. Like a choke collar, a lead should be on the pup only when under your observation.

Continue Teaching Its Name

Couple the pup's name with all commands, saying it before giving the command. Using its name should get the pup's attention, alerting it that you are about to say something meaningful. And later, when you are hunting two dogs together, the proper dog will respond to your command.

Continue Teaching the Pup to Come

Your pup should come when you call its name followed by the "come" command. At first, kneel to the pup's level (play position), clap your hands, and use an excited voice tone. Pick times when the pup is not distracted and is likely to respond correctly. If the pup starts to balk at this fun approach, and it will, use the lead or check cord to influence it. Do not drag the pup, but use a tug to start it toward you, and repeat as needed. Vary the "come" command with a single whistle blast, using the whistle sparingly and only when compliance is ensured. The "come" whistle must be regarded by your pup as serious; it may save the animal's life someday. Later, response to the whistle may be further engrained with proper use of an e-collar and the help of a competent pro. Always praise when the pup comes to you. Coming to you must be a reward. Never punish a pup that has come to you.

Directional work or quartering at an early age is fun for the pup and becomes highly useful later.

Quartering

Too many handlers ignore this command. To my way of thinking, a gun dog that does not quarter efficiently in front of you is worthless. You will use quartering along with the "this way" command for at least four different functions as training progresses. First, you will use it repetitively to teach the dog a quartering motion from right to left and back again as a regular hunting pattern. Second, you will use it to direct the dog when you are changing direction in the field. Third, you will use it to direct the dog to certain desired pieces of cover. Fourth, you will combine it with "fetch" to show the dog the area of a blind fall and direct it to "hunt dead" in that area until it finds the bird. All of these things will come together later, after the dog has learned individual commands and is ready for more advanced training.

Now put the pup on the longer lead or check cord. Pick an object in the distance, and in your mind, draw a straight line to it and a zigzag line using the straight line as a centerline. This is the pattern you are going to teach. Walk fast or jog to the right, calling "this way" and signaling with an outstretched arm. Use the check cord only if necessary to bring the pup along. Stop suddenly, call "this way," and signal back to the left. Again, use the check cord only if necessary to influence the pup. At first the pup will likely follow you out of excitement, probably getting underfoot and wanting to play. That's okay; it will get more focused with time and experience. The important thing is to teach what the directional signal means. Once you are in the field and pup gets into birds, it will start to look like something. For now your goal in the yard is to progress to where you can walk the straight centerline and have the pup quarter right to left and back again in front of you.

I feel that quartering is second only to "come" in importance as a field command. Together the two will produce an efficient worker in the field. Range control is a product of these two commands. It is a combination of heredity and training. If your pup is a less active one and does not take well to quartering, you can delay this for a while. Use your judgment, but do not ignore this command altogether. A first-year dog should come to voice and whistle, quarter to voice and whistle, be staunch on point, and accept the gun. The last two are yet to come.

I use a two-blast whistle for "this way," and along with one blast for "come," these are the only two whistle signals I use. Like the "come" whistle, the two-blast can later be reinforced with the e-collar, but only with the help of a competent pro. A finished dog should turn and come immediately on one blast and change direction immediately on two.

Play Retrieving and the Conditioned Retrieve

Do not be misled by the terminology "play retrieving." You will be teaching the commands associated with retrieving and requiring proper response. "Play retrieving" is used to describe your demeanor and distinguish this from force training. You will be testing the pup's natural instinct to pick up and carry and teaching it by association to pick up and carry on command. Also, you will be teaching with the use of the "come" command to bring the object to you. Many pups naturally pick up and carry, so the owner does not bother teaching retrieving. This is a mistake for two reasons. First, if problems develop later in bird training, you will not have any learned commands to fall back on. Second, when you ask your pup to hunt dead and retrieve on a blind fall, you will have no commands

Natural instinct, repetition, and positive reinforcement are important. Play retrieving with your pup without force is fun and helps develop a dependable retriever. BOTTOM PHOTO: ROBERT WARNER

Natural instinct, repetition, and positive reinforcement are important. Play retrieving with your pup without force is fun and helps develop a dependable retriever.

to use. Most well-bred gun dogs should have some instinct to pick up and carry. By refining it, you can avoid the necessity for force breaking later. Every dual-type setter I have owned has become a reliable retriever through this method.

At first keep it fun. Your demeanor should be different than with obedience work. Continue to work on retrieving from this age until beginning bird work in the field, then drop it, and come back to it only when the first bird is shot over an older, staunch youngster. With a pointing dog, never use bird scent, wings, or anything associated with birds during puppy retrieving. That will come only after the dog is staunch and has had birds killed over it. Puppy play retrieving will not advance as far with a pointing dog as it would with a retrieving breed, but your pup will learn to search for, pick up, and bring back a dummy on command.

Use a small dummy, tennis ball, or stuffed sock, increasing the size of the object as the pup grows. Do not use anything the pup has regular access to or is allowed to chew. In early sessions, toss the dummy close by after getting the pup excited about it. Increase the distance of your tosses as the pup can handle it. Keep the pup on the check cord in case you must use it to coax the animal to you. Do not allow the pup to chew and play with the dummy. Once the pup has brought the dummy to you, encourage it to sit, and praise the pup while allowing it to hold the dummy.

Only three commands are needed: "fetch," "come," and "drop." At first the "fetch" command will follow the natural behavior of picking up and carrying. Then by association, it will eventually precede the behavior, and your pup will have learned to pick up and carry on command. If a pup will pick up and carry naturally, the rest of the retrieving process is your responsibility. Coming to you and delivering is training, because in the wild, the dog would bury or eat its prey. Timing is critical. As soon as the pup picks up the dummy, use your "come" command, preferably the whistle, and then encourage it to come to you by kneeling, using the check cord, or turning and moving hurriedly away. Moving away while commanding "come" presents the pup with a dilemma. It has this object in its mouth that it wants, and you are leaving. Might as well go with the master and bring this thing along. It works nearly every time. When the pup gets close to you, gain control. Get the pup to sit if you can, and praise it profusely. Allow the pup to hold the dummy while you praise, then command "drop" when the pup seems tired of holding it. Keep it fun, and strongly reinforce the act of bringing the dummy to you. Once this simple play procedure is well engrained, you can proceed.

During the process, there are two absolute don'ts you need to be aware of. Do not approach the pup when it is in the act of retrieving, ever. This could cause short stopping or even a complete stoppage of retrieving. The pup may see it as a threatening gesture. Do not rip the dummy away as soon as the pup brings it to you. Again, you may cause short stopping, or an assertive pup may rip back, leading to a hard mouth. This needs to be an enjoyable experience for which you lavishly praise the pup.

If the initial play retrieving goes well and the pup accepts some structure, you can start to "whoa" the pup when throwing the dummy. Do not proceed to this step, however, until you have taught the pup "whoa" as a separate command. More advanced retrieving will be covered later. Remember to stop retrieving work when live bird work begins, and do not resume until the pup is staunch and has had birds killed over it. If play retrieving went well, your pup will probably start to retrieve birds shortly after you start shooting them. At that time, you simply use the commands you taught in play retrieving. If the pup responds, you are on your way. Either way, toss the bird a few times and replicate the work done with the dummy in the yard. Often the act of tossing the bird as you did the dummy triggers the correct response in the pup. If the pup does not catch on, you can go back to the yard and use the dummy with wings attached. Next, go into the field with the winged dummy. Finally, go into the field with a dead bird, toss it, and use a blank gun. Notice that you are getting closer to the real thing by changing only one part of the lesson at a time. This will fill in the gap between a tossed dummy in the yard and a shot bird in the field.

If the pup does not catch on to retrieving during its first season, you may need to take another approach. A pup that will pick up and carry, however, will retrieve without force-breaking. If a pup does not have the instinct and shows no interest in picking up and carrying, you may need to have it force-broken, but do not do so before exhausting the natural approach. Much of this is determined by the pup's breed, bloodline, and individual temperament.

Play Sight Pointing

Play sight pointing of a bird wing can be a fun game with your young pup, and it can help enhance and showcase the pointing instinct. If over-done, however, it can cause major problems later in your pup's training. This is a sight exercise, unlike the scent pointing your pup will be doing in the field on real birds. Doing too much sight pointing, or doing it too late into the pup's age development, can create a sight-dependent pup. Later, when scenting birds in the field, the pup will creep closer in an attempt to see the bird and bust it. This can be a difficult habit to break if allowed to develop. Therefore, if you play this game, do it only occasionally, and stop altogether at about four months or when starting live bird training, whichever comes first.

For this game, you need the tip section of a fishing rod, heavy monofilament line, and a bird wing. Lay and dangle the wing well in front of the pup. Most pups will chase at first, before flashing a point or cat-walking and stalking it. Gently encourage your pup with a verbal command to hold point, and then praise it. After a moment, fly the wing away; do not allow the pup to catch the wing. Some pups will be impressive on this exercise, but others will not point at all. Do not be concerned

Ten-week-old pup sight-pointing a bird wing, provoking its natural instinct.

if your pup will not point the wing. This does not mean it won't be a strong pointer on scent later.

Daily Living Commands

"Get in," "get down," and "get up" are daily living commands that should be started early and used consistently from eight weeks on. You teach them during the normal course of time spent with your pup around the house, yard, or kennel.

Use the "get in" command every time you put the pup into its crate or kennel or let it in the house door. The pup may require a boost when first introduced to a new situation, but it will soon catch on. The command can be used in a multitude of situations and makes control of the pup much more pleasant when it needs to be crated or kenneled for any reason. Separate commands for these various situations are not necessary and only complicate training. If you are standing by a crate, kennel, or doorway, pointing and commanding "get in," any dog should be able to understand the intention.

Every time the pup jumps up or puts its front paws on something, firmly put it down and command "get down." If the pup is larger or older, a knee in the chest at the moment it rears up along with the command "get down" may be necessary. The pup will be off balance on its rear legs, so the impact need not be violent. Have the pup sit, then praise. You will be replacing an undesirable behavior with a desirable one and praising. Your pup will also be learning to sit for praise in training, so eventually it will stop the undesirable behavior and start sitting for praise and attention. A more severe approach for older problem jumpers is to use a limber switch across the front legs when the dog starts up, again commanding "get down" and using the replacement behavior. Do not use anything heavy or stiff that could injure the dog; your intent is simply to correct the behavior. As always, use merely enough force to get the job done, no more, no less.

Early whoa work on the table without force. ROBERT WARNER

"Get up" should be taught only after jumping is broken, so the pup learns to jump just on command. You may choose to not teach this command at all, but I use it frequently for a variety of functions. Simply tap your lap, the grooming table, or truck tailgate while commanding "get up." If necessary, lift the pup's front paws into place. During the pup's growing months, I only allow the pup to put its front paws up, and then I boost it the rest of the way, with my arm between its back legs. I always lift the pup down, as jumping down can cause serious injury to the front shoulders.

The process of breaking jumping, then allowing it only on command, further puts you in control of your pup's behaviors. This is an application of basic-training philosophy.

Grooming Table

My pups are on the grooming table virtually every day of their lives, starting at seven weeks. This exercise will serve many functions throughout their lives. First, it desensitizes the pup to having its ears, eyes, feet, and other body parts handled in a soothing manner. This allows me to do all of my own grooming and caretaking, from trimming, to clipping nails, to caring for minor injuries. Not only do the dogs learn to tolerate these things, but they love the attention. After any field excursion, you should check for injuries, ticks, burs, and other potential problems. If your pup is accustomed to the handling, it will cooperate completely. I also use the table as another training opportunity, working on "stay" ("whoa") every day.

In addition, it is still another opportunity to bond with your pup. Pups jump to be close to your face. This allows them that opportunity, and they come to love it. The more you stroke and handle your pup in a positive, reassuring manner, the more you are building its self-confidence.

Remember, anything you want your pup to do and feel comfortable with needs to be introduced early and often in its life.

THREE TO FIVE MONTHS

Your pup has now begun to learn some very important commands and behaviors. Its attention span should be getting longer and more intent. It is now time to begin more advanced work. From three to five months, your pup will be learning to sit, sit/stay, stand/stay (whoa), and heel. You will also be improving on the commands it already learned.

Sit

There are a variety of ways to approach sit, sit/stay and whoa. Before beginning to teach your pup to sit, read this and the next two sections. After reading all three, you can decide which approach you prefer, then come back and begin with sit, modifying it as explained in the next section if you want to teach sit with the implied stay.

Start by giving the verbal command "sit" while grasping the top of your pup's collar or directly under the neck. At the same time, depress the hindquarters with your other hand. You can gradually eliminate pressure on the hindquarters (you will feel when it is time) and then collar pressure, substituting an upward tug on the lead. Soon the verbal command will be sufficient, and your pup has learned to sit. With some of the more stubborn breeds or individuals, you may need a choke chain, keeping upward pressure on the lead until the pup sits, then immediately releasing pressure. The pup soon learns that sitting relieves the pressure and begins to cooperate.

One of the prevailing myths about training a pointing dog is that you should never teach it to sit for fear it will later sit when on point or when hearing the pointing command, "whoa." This is pure nonsense! Give me any number of dogs to teach to whoa, half having been taught to sit and half not, and equal numbers of each group will sit or drop on the "whoa command" if improperly handled. The likely candidates for this behavior are the more sensitive breeds and individuals. They are responding to the pressure being placed on them. The key is to properly teach the stationary whoa first, then use a soothing, almost two-syllabic "whoa" command.

Because you have purchased this manual, I assume your pup is going to be a companion gun dog, not a field-trial or show prospect. Learning to sit is an integral part of good manners around the house and neighborhood. If your dog is going to be confined to a kennel, and I hope not, then the "sit" command is not as vital.

Sit/Stay

There are two methods of teaching a dog to sit and stay. One is to teach sit with an implied stay, meaning that when teaching sit, you do not allow the pup to move until it is released with the "okay" command, thus eliminating the use of the "stay" command in the sitting position. The other method is to use two separate commands, "sit" and "stay." One reason

Learning sit/stay at an early age is part of companion-dog manners.

ROBERT WARNER

for using the first method is so you can use "stay" for your pointing command. If you teach sit/stay first, there will be some initial confusion if you then use "stay" instead of "whoa" for your pointing command. Using sit with the implied stay also simplifies training, which I am most always in favor of doing. I have always used "stay" instead of "whoa" for pointing, and I have used both methods for teaching a dog to sit and stay. When training for customers, I use any number of approaches to this part of their pup's training. In recent years, I have taken to the implied stay approach and am pleased with the results in my dogs.

It's also important to teach the "okay" command. When releasing your pup from "sit/stay," "whoa," "heel," or any other continuing command,

Whoa work on the ground with no gimmicks during the early months.

ROBERT WARNER

you need to clearly command "okay." This is as important as the initial command.

The technique for teaching stay in the sitting position is the same regardless of which terminology you have chosen. Command "sit" or "sit/stay," then use your hands in front of the pup's face and over its hindquarters, putting the animal back in the original position any time it attempts to move. Your initial goal is to teach the concept that the pup does not move until you command "okay." Time and distance are not important at first. Teach the concept, then go for longer periods of time, staying close to the pup. When your pup starts holding for longer periods of time, you can start to increase the distance between the two of you. It will be a battle of wills at first, but be persistent. Once a pup has learned the concept, increase the level of difficulty, always remaining in position to immediately correct any breakdown. A raised, outstretched hand or finger can be used as a signal to reinforce the verbal command and hold the pup's attention. Increase and vary the difficulty, walking around in front of the pup, and then doing a complete circle around it. Eventually, disappear around the corner and have someone assist you by creating a distraction. With every new wrinkle, be in position to correct any movement, reestablishing the pup in its original place and position. At first it may also help to go back to the pup and physically touch it when releasing it with "okay." Vary this approach by releasing with "okay," then calling the pup to you with the "come" command. As always, the pup must be on a lead and under your control.

When you start using "sit/stay" and "come" together, you are learning how commands will build and combine in a fully trained pup one day. Always praise your pup when it comes to you, no matter what transpired just prior to that. Praise should be measured and fit the accomplishment. Pups that are coddled or berated will not respond well. Stay even, and adjust your emotional output to the situation.

Sit/stay with juvenile and owner.

Never use the "stay" command if you are not going to be around to enforce it. I repeatedly see people who are leaving the house tell the dog to stay as they go out the door. You cannot do that; the key to "stay," "whoa," or any other continuing command is that the pup does not move until you release it. Never give a command you cannot enforce!

Whoa, Hold, or Stay

This is another approach to teaching sit, stay, and whoa. There are various reasons for deviation from the old standard approach. The most common is the fear that a companion dog that is accustomed to hearing "no" around the house will mistake the "whoa" command when on bird scent, and obvious problems could arise. Whichever approach you take, "whoa" is a command of absolute importance. Staunchness, steadiness to wing, steadiness to wing and shot, stopping to flush, and backing are all dependent on this command.

For years I taught my own setters to sit/stay, stand/stay, and lie down/stay with no problems. They learned that "stay" means to hold whatever position they are in when the command is delivered. Recently, I have started using the sit with implied stay approach, reserving "stay" for the pointing stance only. It simplifies the command structure for the pup and avoids early confusion when using "stay" in the pointing position. I am one of those who prefer not to use "whoa." For my training clients, I will teach whatever commands they desire. Most of the time it is "sit/stay" along with either "whoa" or "hold."

If you are training your own pup and have it from seven or eight weeks old, you have plenty of time to use either technique. If you obtain an older dog or have only a short time to instill commands, it is probably better to take the more traditional approach of "sit/stay" and "whoa" or "hold." The quickest method is probably sit with the implied stay and the command "whoa," "hold," or "stay" for pointing. Any of these techniques will work. The important thing is to pick one and stay with it. Be consistent! There are as many ways to train a bird dog as there are bird dogs and owners.

Whichever terminology you choose, the lesson is the same: your pup must stand perfectly still when commanded to do so and not move until released. Start teaching the pointing stance by placing the pup in the standing position and commanding "whoa," "hold," or "stay." I start this exercise on the grooming table and over food even before introducing it into formal training sessions. Use one hand under the abdomen and the other under the neck to gently pull forward and up, placing the pup in the proper standing position. Give your command, and do not allow the pup to move until you say "okay." As when teaching "sit/stay," it will take a while for the pup to understand what you expect from it. Repetition and patience are essential. Give the pup all the help it needs, holding it in position at first, until commanding "okay." Once it has learned the concept you can move your hands away and expect longer time periods first, then more distance. "Whoa" means the pup may not move a muscle until you release it; if it does, place it back in the original position and repeat the command. If pup is allowed to make the decision when to move, it will never be staunch or steady.

Once your pup has learned the command in the stationary position, start to teach it on the move. Keep your pup on the lead and close by at first. When the pup has a natural inclination to stop and watch something, take advantage by giving your "whoa" command and using the lead to influence the pup. If your pup does not stop and hold, get to it, place it in position, again command "whoa," and release with "okay." Continue until the pup will stop and hold on its own, then lengthen the distance between you gradually. Eventually you should be able to stop a pup in full stride with the "whoa" command and hold until released. As this process is under way, continue to reinforce the command on the grooming table and over food.

Through all of this training, voice inflection is critical. Think of how your pup responds when you shout "no" loudly for a wrongdoing: It will usually drop or sit in shame. You do not want this reaction when teaching "whoa." First, be sure the pup fully understands the command in the stationary position before teaching it on the move. Second, when delivering this command, be particularly soothing, almost making the word two-syllabic. A soothing delivery with a lot of stroking and positive reinforcement will achieve good results. If a dog drops on "whoa," this is a response to pressure and is most common in sensitive dogs.

Be sure this command is well engrained in the yard before using it in the field around birds. You want your pup to be confident and self-assured, and not to be alarmed by hearing a new command associated only with birds. This command is critical for pointing dogs.

Whichever approach you have used to teach these three steps, the result should be the same: your dog should have learned to stay while sitting or standing until released. Learning to sit and stay is a nicety for manners around the house and neighborhood. "Whoa," "hold," or "stay" is an essential field command and thus the most important. Because I use "stay" instead of "whoa" or "hold" as a pointing command, I will refer to it as such throughout the remainder of the text.

Continue Teaching the Pup to Come

Continue to teach the "come" command, introducing distractions and increasingly difficult situations. As your pup ages, it may start to balk. If this begins to happen, use an increasingly longer check cord, reminding the pup that no matter how free it thinks it may be, it is not. You are omnipresent! If you have not done so previously, you should introduce the single-whistle blast now, using it only during strict training, and always enforcing it to the letter. Do not call your pup repeatedly when it is not responding and is not on a check cord; you will teach it that it does not have to come. Remember, never give a command you cannot enforce!

Lie Down/Stay

Here again there are two approaches: If you used the implied stay approach with "sit," you can do the same with "lie down." If you used "stay" with "sit," you can do the same with "lie down." With the pup in the sitting position, sweep the front legs from under it and gently press down on the hindquarters while giving the command. If you want to add a hand signal, lower your open hand toward the ground in front of the pup's face.

This command is another that serves you around the house and has no real application in the field. I use it when at the dinner table. I command my dogs to "lie down/stay" in the adjacent room, and they remain there until released at the end of the meal.

Heel

"Heel" can be one of the more difficult obedience commands to teach, and it necessitates putting some pressure on the pup. For this reason, you should wait until around five months of age to start teaching it. It will be one of the last obedience commands you introduce.

To teach your pup to heel, begin with the leashed pup sitting at your left side. Hold the lead across your body, below belt level, with the end in your right hand and guided by the left hand. Command "heel" and start walking in a straight line, influencing the pup with a tug on the lead. If the pup wanders to the front or side, jerk the lead in toward your knee hard enough to get the animal back in the proper position, command "heel" again, and immediately release the pressure on the lead. Continue walking in a straight line while doing this. Do not jerk up on the lead; lead pressure must be in toward your left knee. Do not maintain a tight lead; the release is what teaches your pup the proper response. If you maintain constant pressure, the pup will pull back, and a tug-of-war will result. It is vital to jerk hard enough to get the pup back into position, relax the pressure, and continue walking. Jerk and relax, jerk and relax,

Heeling as a juvenile, the last obedience command taught.

jerk and relax. The better you perform this lead technique, the sooner the pup will start to heel without pressure. Otherwise, the tug-of-war could go on forever. The pup's head should be at the side of your knee so that it can see you stop or turn and respond appropriately. At first, walk in a straight line for only a short distance. Start from sit/heel and end with sit/heel, repeating the short spurts over and over. With time, increase the distance and start doing turns.

Next, teach your pup the automatic sit at the end and the automatic come-around to start. The automatic sit at the end is easily taught by exaggerating your stop, tugging up on the lead, and commanding "sit." Soon the tug will be enough, and eventually the sit will be automatic. The automatic come-around at the beginning starts with the pup sitting facing you. Command "heel," and influence the pup around your right with the lead in your right hand. Switch hands on the lead behind your back, and influence the pup forward along your left side with lead pressure and a forward step. When pup is on your left side, tug up on the lead and command "sit." I like to tap my left thigh as a hand signal for this command. With repetition, your pup will soon come around behind you and assume the heel/sit position on command.

Once your pup learns the basics of heeling—coming to the heel/sit position, walking with its head beside your knee without pressure, and ending with the stop/sit—you can start the figure eight and combine the "heel," "sit," and "come" commands into one routine. From the heel/sit starting position, begin walking your pup in a figure eight, making an inside turn on one end of the eight and an outside turn on the other end. Occasionally stop/sit and walk away, turning to face the pup at lead distance. From there, call the pup to you, commanding "sit" when it gets there. With the pup sitting facing you, command "heel," have it execute the come-around and sit/heel, and praise it. Start over, and do as many repetitions as necessary.

Once the pup is catching on to the figure-eight routine, you can use it as a daily review of "heel," "sit/stay," and "come." Any of these commands that are weak can still be worked on separately. Eventually start dropping the lead and allowing the pup to drag it while heeling. If the pup wanders, correct it by stepping on the lead or picking it up. Keep working on this until the pup will do the figure-eight routine while dragging the lead without correction. Finally, have it do the figure-eight routine off-lead.

This is a gradual process that will take weeks to teach. Any time your pup has trouble with a new progression, go back to the previous step and repeat before moving ahead again. As with all commands, make sure the pup is reliable in an isolated environment before introducing distractions. Off-lead obedience is evidence to you and the pup that it is fully trained on that command. Never use it to show off and put your pup in a potentially dangerous situation, such as around traffic.

The "heel" command is useful in many situations in and out of the field. Always carry a lead in your vehicle and your hunting vest, but if for some reason you do not have one on you, heeling can be valuable. It can be used for crossing country roads, approaching good cover across an open area, going through a barnyard full of animals, passing other hunters with dogs, and other situations in the field where control is essential. With maturity and proper handling, your pup will learn to heel in these and other situations off-lead. Again, recognize that any new situation offers a challenge to your training. Anticipate breakdowns, and be ready to reinforce the proper response before the pup has a chance to fail.

Retrieving

Do not force your pup at this time; retrieving should be fun. If the pup is progressing well and you have not started live bird work, continue to play retrieve in the yard. At this point, you may be able to start teaching your pup to whoa while you throw the dummy. To do this, stand on the check cord behind the pup while commanding "stay" or "whoa." If the pup breaks when you throw the dummy—and it will—allow the check cord to do the work. Do not say anything, and do not involve yourself in the correction at all. When the pup is stopped, pick it up, put it back in the stand/stay position, and then send it for the dummy using the "fetch" command. Be positive and soothing in handling the pup in this exercise. If the pup balks in going for the dummy after being corrected, go back to the previous stage and build more enthusiasm. Your pup is not ready for control yet in this exercise.

Retrieving is a secondary instinct in pointing dogs, but it can be encouraged and enhanced if you pay attention to your pup's readiness stages. A well-bred gun dog can become a reliable retriever without force-breaking, contrary to some modern ideas. If your pup will stand/stay and retrieve on command, you can progress to facing the pup and tossing the dummy right or left, associating the hand signal when sending it and commanding "fetch." Eventually you can hide the dummy and use your hand signal and "fetch" command to start teaching the pup to hunt dead.

Quartering

Continue to use voice, whistle, and hand signals to teach quartering. By now you should be able to walk in a straight line across the yard while casting the pup right to left, left to right, and so on. If more room is needed, take the pup into a cut field where there are no birds, and use a longer check cord. If there are natural barriers on each side of the strip you are using, they can aid in teaching the pup to change directions.

Quartering is overlooked by many trainers, but next to "whoa," it is your most important field command. Many field-trial breeders and trainers discourage it and instead encourage running a line. In consistent cover, however, running a line renders a dog almost worthless.

Remember, you are developing a companion gun dog, not an all-age horseback trial dog. Your dog should adjust its range to suit the cover but still be quartering and checking on you.

CHAPTER FOUR

Early Field Training

As soon as your pup is old enough, take it for short fun walks in the field and begin to introduce it to birds. I usually start bird work when my pups are about five months of age, depending on the individual and the time of year. At first you are just out for a short romp. Keep it fun, be positive, and allow the pup to broaden its horizons. Change direction a lot, use your quartering and "come" commands, and encourage the pup when it responds to your handling. Remember, this is a companion gun-dog prospect, and you are starting to develop a working partnership.

Bird Work

The most important part of the pup's early field sessions is to introduce it to birds and bring out its natural bird drive. Use either wild birds or strong-flying liberated birds in these first encounters. The pup's first bird encounters should be as natural as possible. I like to jump-start the pup by releasing a quail from a carry pen in front of it so that the pup can both see and smell the bird. From there, we go for a walk in the field and either find that bird or others that have been released in the field previously. Quail are excellent for the pup's first contacts. They are generally low fliers for a short distance. This gets the pup excited and chasing, bringing out the bird drive.

Your first task is to get the pup deliberately using its nose and searching for scent. Next, your pup should start to naturally show-point, either by flash-pointing and flushing or by catwalking and stalking before flushing. Allow the pup to chase a short distance to build interest, but do not allow it to chase indefinitely. If the pup will stop chasing and come when called, bring it back to the spot of the flush and command "stay" or "whoa" in a reassuring, positive manner. When releasing the pup, take it in a different direction from where the bird flew. As the pup gets bolder, you may have to drag a check cord. Do not use it in a corrective manner

Ginger sitting to deliver at two years.

39

Juvenile setter pointing one of her first scent birds. CHUCK WEAVER

at this age; simply use it to ease the pup to a stop before calling it back to the place of the flush. Do not handle the pup on birds yet, only after the fact. This will help discourage chasing and encourage the pup's natural inclination to point.

Once the pup's bird drive is elevated, you can start to introduce it to the gun. You can start to verbally whoa the pup when it shows point. Do not physically handle the pup yet, and flush the bird as quickly as possible. Too much handling, pressure, and artificial conditions can cause some pups to worry and become potential blinkers. Your pup needs to have many bird contacts, show strong natural pointing instinct, and be more advanced before attempting to work on staunchness. During this time, you are still working on "stay" ("whoa") in the yard, on the grooming table, over food, and so on.

At first, the chasing of other animals should not be dealt with too severely. Ideally, you can get the pup into sufficient numbers of birds before it encounters other game and nongame animals. The pup's temperament and propensity to chase should be considered at all times. Lack of interest on your part or mild reprimands may be enough to discourage such chasing. Building interest in birds and rewarding the pup will help override any potential interest in other game, and once its bird drive is high enough, you can get more insistent that it not chase unwanted game. My pups have hundreds of bird contacts and dozens killed over them before they are ever put in a real hunting situation. For those of us who are grouse hunters, deer chasing is the worst possible sin, but it is more easily prevented than corrected. Proper introduction to birds and solid obedience training hold the key to prevention.

After your pup is pointing with intensity, has had sufficient bird contacts, and begins to mature some, you can begin to handle it on point. When this happens is entirely up to the pup's temperament and the number of bird contacts. For most pups, it will come within a month or two of beginning field training. Do not be impatient or push too hard too soon. There is no hurry; you will be together for the next twelve years or so. Use good judgment, and seek professional help if you are not sure how to proceed. Birds and gun introduction are critical events in your pup's young life. Many amateur handlers need help with these tasks. Be sure to select a trainer that is suited to your dog's type, breed, and bloodline.

Your entire first season will require patience and sacrifice. I am always reminded of the road signs at construction sites, "Temporary Inconvenience for Permanent Improvement."

INTRODUCING THE GUN

There are a number of ways for an experienced pro to introduce pups to gunfire; however, there is one surefire manner for the amateur handler to introduce the gun. Why take chances? Gun-shy dogs are made, not born! Sensitive pups are more likely to have problems if not introduced properly, but gun shyness is a learned trait. As with blinking and deer chasing, it makes sense to avoid the problem from the outset rather than having to cure it later. Breaking an already gun-shy dog is a long, tedious process requiring plenty of birds, time, and patience. It will not be necessary if you introduce the gun properly to begin with.

Do no gun work until your pup has developed a high level of intensity around birds and is chasing with enthusiasm on flush. The pup may or may not be showing point yet, but it should be fired up about birds and bird scent. Begin by firing one round of a light crimp blank, not much louder than a child's cap pistol, when the pup is chasing a flushed bird and is a good distance out in front of you. You may want to muffle the sound even more by holding the gun behind your back. At first you are counting on the pup's bird interest to override the noise of the gun, so the pup must be chasing and intent on the bird. A bold pup may not notice the sound at all, but a sensitive one may be overly concerned. A pup's normal reaction is to stop and look just to see what it was. Your role is to continue as if nothing happened. If you are unconcerned, the normal pup will be unconcerned. If the pup overreacts, stop using the gun and do more bird work. Try again after the pup experiences more birds and exhibits greater boldness.

If your pup shows a normal reaction, proceed with caution. Fire the crimp blank on some flushes, closer to the pup as you proceed. If the timing works out as usual on this, your pup will be pointing and holding longer at the same time it is accepting the gun. When it all comes together, the pup will hold point until you flush the bird and fire the crimp blank at the bird as in actual hunting. When this happens, you are ready to kill a bird or two over your youngster in a controlled situation.

At this point, you will need an assistant who is a good shot. Use a light load, and do not miss! Guide the pup into the bird, and keep it on point while your assistant flushes and kills the bird. You want to take a fail-safe approach so that the pup's first experience with the real thing is a positive one. Doing this on a couple of birds will put the entire picture together for the pup. From here you will go back and work on staunchness in the pup as needed before hunting it for real. Handling should be minimal, possibly only picking up the check cord and holding it tight while the bird is flushed and shot. Encourage the pup to retrieve, using the commands you taught in yard training: "fetch," "come," and "drop."

If the pup makes the retrieve, toss the bird a few more times as in yard retrieving, and praise profusely. You want to engrain this positive response thoroughly. If the pup is confused and makes only a partial retrieve or none at all, it's okay. The gun, blood, scent, and freshly killed bird are a long way from retrieving a dummy in the yard. Pick up the bird and try to encourage the pup by tossing it and play retrieving as in the yard. Often this will trigger a positive response. Continue to toss killed birds, encourage the pup to retrieve, and praise when it does. If the pup is

One-year-old Wildcherry, staunch on a training bird.

still confused, it is not unusual. It may take some time and some advanced yard training to close the gap between a dummy in the yard and a freshly killed bird. If your pup showed an instinct to pick up and carry a dummy in the early play retrieving sessions, it will retrieve reliably without force-breaking. It just takes birds, patience, and proper technique.

If you have followed the schedule and your pup has progressed normally, this should all start to come together around seven or eight months of age. Do not be alarmed, however, if your pup progresses at a different speed. All pups are different, and all handlers have various skill levels. Continue to work on staunchness, occasionally killing birds for your pup as a reward. Shoot only pointed birds; do not shoot mistakes. If hunting season is on, take the pup hunting and kill birds for it. Do not overtrain or overhandle the pup on birds. Though your pup may be ready to do some hunting, it is by no means finished. The entire first season will be a learning process for your pup and a training exercise for you.

STAUNCHNESS ON POINT

Though your pup may have been staunch enough, with some help, for you to kill a couple of birds for it, that does not mean it is reliably staunch no matter what. Your goal now is to work toward staunchness. This can be greatly accelerated with judicious use of strong flying pen birds and remote launchers. Pen birds may not be necessary if you live in an area with high concentrations of wild birds, but they allow you to control the situation and to get done in minutes what may take days in the wild. Once pups have progressed to this point, I get away from quail and go to stronger- and higher-flying chukars and homing pigeons. I use pigeons in launchers when not shooting, which allows me to take the pup off the check cord and hunt naturally. If the pup points and holds, I launch the bird and fire the blank gun. The pup cannot catch a launched, high-flying pigeon and will soon learn this. Use your whistle to call the pup back, put it on point at the original site, and praise. Release the pup and head away from the direction in which the bird flew.

If the pup points and starts, launch the bird immediately and command "stay" ("whoa"). The flushing bird will serve as a self-correcting mechanism, just like a wild bird, and your command will replace the improper break with a positive experience, further reinforcing staunchness. If you do not have launchers or pigeons, the same technique will work on a bumped game bird, using a check cord to help control the pup. When the pup points and holds staunchly, I replace the pigeons with chukars and reward it with a kill and retrieve. Switching back and forth from positive to negative reinforcement will soon teach the pup that staunchness is rewarded with praise and possibly a kill. A lack of staunchness will be corrected, and no reward will be forthcoming.

When using pen birds, some cautions are in order. First, be sure they are strong fliers; never allow the pup to catch one. Second, wear gloves when handling birds and launchers. You cannot totally eliminate human scent, but you can noticeably reduce it. Third, try to place birds in favorable scenting conditions and positions. I try to pick breezy conditions when working set birds, and I place them in an elevated position where I can work the pup uphill into descending scent. It helps them to learn to pick up their nose and to point at greater distances. Finally, do not do too

Male pointer showing style in point. MARIO T. EUSI

much handling at this stage. Try to simulate the real thing by getting the bird into the air with dispatch. When flushing birds for any dog, circle out and come in at a right angle where the dog can see you. This will reassure the pup and help hold it on point. The surest way to unnerve any dog on point is to sneak up from behind and pass it. This will encourage creeping.

When working on birds, maintain the same emotional level as in yard training. Any time you leave your emotional base, the pup will notice, and the resulting response could be a potential problem. Be assertive, positive, and reassuring around birds, as elsewhere. Handle on birds only enough to achieve staunchness. Too much handling and correction can soften the pup on birds and even lead to bird shyness or blinking.

At this point, the pup will still chase on flush. A certain amount of this is okay; you are not going to steady a first-year pup. If you have been using the recall and reestablishing point, most pups will learn to come back when whistled or when the bird is not shot. If this becomes a problem, consult a pro for help. Throughout the first season, do not shoot bumped birds, unless you want your pup to become a flushing dog, and always take time to call the pup back and reestablish the point at the sight of the flush before proceeding in the opposite direction from the bird.

Although genetics and training are of obvious importance, it takes birds, birds, and more birds to make a bird dog. In addition to working with training birds, your pup should have dozens of birds killed over it during the first season. Bird experience and maturity will be the linchpins of finishing training before the second season. Without them, you cannot proceed with finishing your dog. A first-season pup should be staunch, coming to the whistle, quartering to the whistle, and accepting the gun. When those are achieved, take it hunting and have fun!

ADVANCED FIELD QUARTERING

Continue to teach quartering in the field throughout your first-season training. On average, I work a first-year youngster on birds about a third of the time in the field. The other sessions are spent working on handling and response to the come and quartering whistles. At this point, you are still working on the individual building blocks separately while you gradually put it all together.

Using either the check cord or e-collar, dedicate two out of three sessions to handling, building the pup's enthusiasm and drive while teaching it to hunt to the gun. The check cord is still the trainer's number-one tool. When working on quartering, use a long check cord of about seventy-five feet. Hold on to the check cord, and check the pup at the end of each cast. Use the two-blast whistle signal to get the pup's attention, then the hand signal to turn it and bring it back across in front of you. Do this repetitively on every cast up and down the field. Short to medium-length grass with natural edge boundaries works well for this exercise. Change directions and use your two-blast whistle signal to get the pup to change with you.

If the pup lines straight out to the end of the check cord, use the "come" whistle command to start it toward you. Then, when the pup is coming toward you, use the two-blast signal and hand motion to put it back into a quartering action. Give the pup positive verbal reinforcement when it responds correctly to your handling. Continue to work on handling during all training and hunting in the pup's first season. Combining handling and bird work will start to develop the pup into a dependable foot-hunting companion gun dog. I concentrate on the dog during its first season, giving up some hunting to do the right thing for the pup's future as a gun dog. Doing so will pay dividends in future seasons in the form of an accomplished gun dog. Be patient, and be thankful you have a pup that will handle and hunt for you, not itself.

For early field training, you will need two lengths of check cords. Buy a hundred-foot cotton clothesline, and cut it into two sections, one of 25 feet for dragging free when working on birds, and one of 75 feet for field quartering. Attach a barrel or French snap to one end, and put a small knot in the other to prevent fraying. Always wear leather gloves when handling your pup on a check cord to avoid rope burns.

Your pup is now obedience trained, and in the field, it comes and quarters to the whistle, is staunch on point, and accepts the gun. You are now ready to start reaping some of the rewards of your labor. This does not mean that your pup is finished or ready to handle everything it encounters in the field. Have fun, but proceed with caution. You have only one chance to experience your pup's first season, and it is better to go slowly than to push too hard.

Try to limit the pup's first trips afield to ones with a high likelihood of success. Keep the hunts relatively short—an hour and a half to two hours is plenty for a developing pup. You could still do structural damage by running the pup into the ground. Hunt alone or with one trustworthy companion who knows you have a young pup and is willing to sacrifice shooting, if necessary. Pick your spots carefully, choosing ones where you can handle the pup with a high degree of success. A lost pup is no fun! Try at first to avoid roads, deer, hunters, and other distractions as much as possible. Your goal is a short trip with a point, kill, and positive reinforcement. Shoot points but not bumped birds, taking the time to use corrective action the same as in your training sessions. Shooting random flushes is a decision to make based on your pup's temperament and level of sophistication. The first season really is advanced training on the real thing.

ADVANCED GUN WORK

Your pup has already been properly introduced to the gun, but it is relatively inexperienced and encounters new situations on each outing. A bad experience with the gun could still create a gun-shy dog. Shooting only pointed birds will protect against this happening, since your pup sees the entire picture and makes the positive association of bird and gun. If you choose to shoot random flushes, be careful. I have already suggested taking no more than one other hunter on your pup's first outings. The more commotion and excitement, the higher the likelihood of a negative

Female setter with Pennsylvania limit of two grouse.

experience. A line of five hunters and a barrage of a dozen shots could ruin your young pup. Be careful—hunt alone or with one reliable partner. Stay close so that your pup is aware of your presence and can quarter in front of both hunters. Even on random flushes, the pup will likely see or hear birds and not be bothered by the gun. Again, never shoot a bumped bird.

To guarantee success, it is best to limit your pup's first exposures to real hunting and the gun. Understand that every new experience brings with it a chance of failure as well as success. The more you can stack the deck on the side of success, the better for your pup. You may sacrifice some chances to kill birds now, but the reward will be future successful seasons. There is only one first season and one chance to do it right the first time around.

POINTING MANNERS AFIELD

Throughout your pup's first season, continue to pay close attention to staunchness on every bird. Continue the same handling techniques as in the training field. When your pup points staunchly, get the bird in the air quickly and kill it. If your pup bumps the bird, put your gun down, call the pup back to the site of the infraction, and tell it "stay" ("whoa") in a reassuring fashion. Have the pup hold for a few seconds, then take it away from the direction of the bird's flight. The combination of having pointed birds shot for it and being corrected on bumped birds will make the pup more staunch as time passes. This technique will also start to plant the seed of steadiness to wing. Do not expect your pup to steady during the first season. A pup handled this way will be easier to hunt with and more ready to begin steadiness training before its second season.

The amount of handling needed will depend on the individual pup's progress. A sensitive pup requires less handling and will not react well to it. A bolder pup may require more handling. In either case, do not be negative around birds. Use the same staunching technique as before when necessary. If necessary and the cover allows it, you may even want to drag a short check cord to facilitate the staunching procedure. You can use it to handle and reinforce correct pointing manners while your partner shoots, or you can use it to stop the pup and get it back if it bumps and chases. If a pup is particularly bold, you can jolt it firmly at the end of the check cord before calling it back and reestablishing point. If pointing man-

One-year-old Blue, staunch on a training bird.

ners break down completely, stop hunting the pup and get back to the training field, pen birds, and a fail-safe approach.

There is a balance between allowing your pup to have fun and maintaining control. You must convince your pup that a proper point will be rewarded with a kill and retrieve. This is the most important lesson your dog will ever learn. A pointing dog that is not staunch is worthless. Throughout your dog's career, always insist on a staunch point, and if there is any doubt, take corrective measures. In review, staunchness means that your pup holds point until the bird flushes. This is the extent of pointing manners for the pup's first season. Steadiness to wing, steadiness to wing and shot, and stopping to flush will be second-season lessons.

RANGE AND HANDLING

Continue to insist on proper quartering and coming responses throughout the pup's first season. I tend to overhandle pups during their first season, wanting to promote success and avoid a lost pup. This may cause a few wild flushes and missed opportunities at birds, but it is for the betterment of the pup.

Use your come and two-blast quartering whistles as in training. The whistle is preferable to your voice because it is less disturbing to birds and carries farther in the woods. Also, your pup has been taught to take it more seriously than your voice. I recommend using the quartering whistle over the come signal nine out of ten times. If the pup is to your right or left, regardless of range, the quartering whistle will probably work well. You do not want to be constantly calling your pup completely in to you. If the pup does line straight out too far, use the come whistle first. When the pup is coming toward you and gets back in acceptable range, give the two-blast whistle and hand signal to put it back into a quartering motion. Save the come signal for absolute situations, when you want the pup to come in to your feet and take a break.

Range is the most often and heatedly debated aspect of a gun dog's training. There is no absolute correct range. Correct range for a pointing dog is highly variable, depending on a number of factors. Pointing dogs should range beyond the gun. They should cover more ground than you would cover alone or with a flushing dog. Range is dictated by the cover, the amount of birds, the age and condition of the hunter, and any number

German shorthair female pointing at eight months.
DONNIE EBERSOLE

of other factors. A good dog will adjust its range to the conditions. In summary, the correct range is far enough to encounter birds and point them before they are alarmed and on the move from hunter noise, yet close enough that the shooter can get to them on point to kill the bird. After all, these are gun dogs.

A properly trained pointing dog will hold point until you arrive on the scene to flush it. Bumping a bird at ten yards is the same fault as bumping one at seventy-five yards and should be dealt with in the same manner. If range and handling become a major problem, deal with this in separate training sessions after the season. If they interfere with your hunting too much, stop hunting the pup and go back to repetitive drill on handling.

Genetics and training play a role in determining your pup's range. In the field, the thickness of the cover and the number of birds also affect range. Thicker cover and more birds will cause the pup to hunt closer; sparse cover and a lack of birds will encourage the pup to reach out. Everyone is comfortable with different distances in a pointing dog. At this point, if you cannot get your pup to hunt at a comfortable range for you, you need to decide whether advanced training will solve the problem or you have to replace your pup. Consult a pro, and if you have not tried an e-collar, it may help.

With luck, if you have chosen from gun-dog stock, the problem may only be one of puppy enthusiasm that can be corrected with training and maturity. I am often confronted by owners who are new to handling pointing dogs and do not understand how a pointing dog should range. Also, control is control, whether the pup is thirty yards out or one hundred. Range and handling problems are probably the most frequent ones I encounter as a trainer. Most often they are not the problem that the owner thinks. On the occasion that they are a real problem, breeding is often the culprit.

In summary, field handling involves two commands properly taught: "come" and quartering. Anything else is unnecessary and extra baggage that will confuse your pup.

ADVANCED RETRIEVING

Losing downed birds is not a pleasant option. Every hunter should go the distance to recover downed birds. A gun dog that hunts dead and retrieves with determination is invaluable. In grouse woods, I feel that a

Rose retrieving the last pheasant of the day for me. JEFF KAUFFMAN

dog that will not retrieve is almost worthless. We would have lost a large number of birds over the years if it were not for my setters.

This is now the real thing; birds that fall stone dead in plain view are a rarity. More often there are blind falls, crippled runners, and hit birds that seemingly fly on. Your job is to mark well and get your dog into position to make the retrieve. If the pup sees the bird fall, chances are its instincts will take over, and you will simply need to use your "come" command to encourage the completed retrieve as in training. Use the same "fetch," "come," and "drop" commands that you taught in the yard and training sessions. If the pup does not see the bird fall, resort to your technique for blind retrieves. Use the two-whistle and hand signal to put the pup in the correct area, then command "fetch." Continue to insist on hunting dead until the bird is found. Do not compete with the dog; once it is in the area and hunting dead, stand still and allow it to do the job it was trained for. The more you move around in the area of the fall, the more you destroy scent for your dog. Also, if you retrieve the bird, the dog is likely to stop doing it. Put your pup in position to do the job, then let it do it. Be sure to give a large amount of praise when the job is completed. You can also do a couple of extra tosses and retrieves to continue engraining the retrieving process. Do not panic if feathers are flying and the dog does a lot of excited mouthing of the bird. This is natural with a youngster and is not likely hardmouth. Also, if the bird is still alive, the pup will have to struggle to get it under control. Never approach your pup in a threatening manner. As soon as the bird is clearly in the pup's mouth, blow your come whistle and move away quickly. Using the whistle will avoid the natural excitement and change of inflection in your voice that could alarm the pup. In addition, if you have trained correctly, the whistle is stronger than your voice and more likely to override the pup's natural excitement. If the pup's instincts are good and you have done your job, retrieving should come together by the end of the first season.

If necessary, continue to work on retrieving in the yard throughout the first season. At this point, you can use a dummy with feathers attached or a dead bird. Keep the pup on the check cord, and continue to use the same techniques and commands. Also, hide the dummy and work on hunting dead using the two-blast whistle and hand signal. A check cord will help guide the pup if it is having trouble. Make sure the pup always finds the dummy and is rewarded. The pup will soon learn to trust your hand signal, finding a dummy or bird every time you point to an area. If the pup is bold, you may be able to stay (whoa) it and send it to retrieve on command. You may even be able to add the blank gun to the training exercise. In this way, you are working on retrieving and planting the seeds for steadiness in the future. How far you advance with this technique depends on your pup. If you begin to stay it and your pup starts to balk at going for the dummy, stop. Go back to allowing the pup to chase on the toss and build enthusiasm.

Retrieving can be a game around the house as well. My Tuck thinks it is his job to retrieve every shoe, sock, and other object left on the floor. He sits and receives praise for doing so, then drops on command. Never discipline a pup for picking up and carrying if you want it to retrieve. This is different from chewing, which does require discipline. Retrieving is icing on the cake for a pointing dog. It is both practical and a source of pride for the dog's handler.

CHASING DEER AND OTHER UNWANTED ANIMALS

If you have started your pup correctly, this should not become a problem. Preventing deer chasing is easier than breaking it and is a matter of training and breeding. Air-scenting dogs will be less likely to develop this problem, but all breeds can be taught to avoid it. First, if your pup is thoroughly obedience trained, you should be able to control it and stop unwanted behaviors more easily. Second, if your pup has had birds well engrained, this will help override other distractions. A dog that has birds on the brain will not be easily distracted from the task at hand, but if it is, you can punish it knowing you will not affect its bird drive. Third, be careful where you take your pup on its first hunts. Pick areas where you can readily keep your pup in view and control it more easily. Fourth, don't be greedy. Killing birds is secondary to keeping your pup on track during this first season.

Deer chasing is a potentially deadly problem in a gun-dog pup. If it does occur, it needs to be dealt with immediately and severely. All pups will naturally chase running or flying game on sight. This is different from dropping their noses and scent-tracking, which is a real problem. If you catch your pup in a sight chase, discipline according to the game and situation. A sight chase and successful correction on the pup's first hunt is sometimes the best thing that can happen. If the pup is allowed to sight-chase, it will eventually start to associate scent and begin to scent-track. Do not allow this to happen! Most deer chasing is the product of an out-of-control pup, away from the master and prone to investigate new and intriguing scents. Keeping your pup under control and in view until it has gained sufficient experience is vital to preventing deer chasing. If a problem develops despite your best efforts, you may want to consult a pro. E-collars are invaluable for breaking deer chasing and much more humane than older techniques.

FIRST-SEASON SUMMARY

Do not expect to have a finished dog at the end of its first season. Have fun, enjoy your pup, expose it to birds, and expect only those results that innate ability and training allow. Careful handling, positive reinforcement, and prevention are the rule for your pup's first season. If numbers of wild birds in your area are not sufficient, you should find a good shooting preserve. It is important to kill a large number of birds to ready your pup for advanced second-season training. There is no substitute for birds and maturity. It takes two full seasons to finish a pointing dog.

Grouse, AyA, and Tuck at sixteen months.

CHAPTER SIX

Shooting Preserves: For the Sake of Your Dog

In my thirty-five years of breeding and training gun dogs and guiding hunters, one of the most prevalent faults I have observed is hunters not killing enough birds over their dogs to realize the animals' full potential. Great bird dogs are the product of quality breeding, conscientious training, and birds. Birds, birds, birds, and more birds are essential to develop a young gun-dog prospect. After starting a youngster for a client, my instructions for the first season include killing birds when the pup does it right and not making shooting mistakes. A minimum of thirty to forty birds need to be killed over the first-year prospect.

To begin finishing that same pup before its second season, a trainer is counting on a degree of emotional maturity and plenty of bird experience to have been achieved during the first season. To teach steadiness to either wing or wing and shot, to teach stopping to flush, and to finish backing manners, much pressure will be put on the second-year prospect. Both emotional maturity and bird drive are needed to keep that prospect from becoming soft and breaking down around birds. Without these two things, blinking could be the worst-case scenario.

Many owners are alarmed at these instructions and perplexed at the prospect of having to kill that many birds over their first-year pup. In many areas of the country, wild bird numbers are not sufficient. In my own area of south-central Pennsylvania, the only wild bird hunting remaining is for ruffed grouse, and the typical hunter is hard-pressed to get even thirty shots at grouse in a season. How can gun-dog owners get their youngster into sufficient numbers of birds? Those who have the means and opportunity may travel to other parts of the country, but others will have to depend on shooting preserves. Yes, shooting preserves!

Being a public school teacher for thirty years, I had limited time to travel in the fall. I have been using shooting preserves for thirty years to

My famous Rose pointing a bird at one year.

Chukar retrieve and presentation at one year.

extend the season from three or four months to eight months, multiplying exponentially the bird opportunities for my dogs. One quality day on a preserve may offer more opportunities than a month of wild bird hunting in our area. To the dogs, it is "real" hunting, but to the handler, it offers a semicontrolled environment in which to refine your dog's manners. What should you look for in a shooting preserve? What opportunities do they offer? How can you approach the hunts so that potential disasters are turned into training opportunities? All these questions and more need to be considered to maximize what preserves have the potential to offer.

Approached without forethought and careful dog handling, the shooting-preserve experience can be a disaster. Birds that do not always act naturally can cause breakdowns in pointing manners and do permanent damage to your pup's progress and behavior around wild birds. By being aware of these possibilities and in position to turn goofy bird behavior into a positive training tool, both you and your dog can benefit. Good preserves offer a variety of birds and experiences, from planting and marking birds for the more inexperienced pup to shooting scratch for the veteran gun dog and owner. Find a preserve that offers quality birds and cover and puts its clients' dogs at the top of its priority list. Poor-flying birds and a mentality that puts killing birds above dog work should be avoided like the plague. In our part of the country, preserve shooting after the season takes place during January, February, and March, meaning cover should be sufficient to hold up through snow and ice and continue to provide quality habitat.

My preference in birds is for huns first, then chukars, with quail and ringnecks coming in last. Chukars offer the most bang for your buck, at a two-for-one cost ratio compared with ringnecks and huns. For the same money, you can get your dog into twice the number of birds, and that is your priority. When in sufficient cover, huns and chukars seem more likely to fly stronger and more easily. Huns can be challenging shooting, even on a preserve. Preserve pheasants can be difficult to get into the air, and quail are often low, weak fliers by comparison. If you are working a first-year pup, you would also be well advised to be careful about using pheasants. A crippled cock pheasant can be hard on a sensitive youngster. A flogging or spurring could leave a lasting impression and have a negative impact on your pup's retrieving.

When working an unfinished youngster on training or preserve birds, you need to take precautions and be a trained observer. A check cord is an essential tool, and a reliable shooter should be along, allowing you to concentrate on handling the pup. Not only should the shooter be accurate, but he or she also should be willing to shoot only those birds that your pup has pointed with your direction. Shooting bumped birds or mistakes will reinforce the negative behavior and encourage its reoccurrence. Your diligent observation is needed to avoid allowing creeping or crowding birds. Though training or preserve birds will tolerate this movement, wild birds will not. This can become a devastating habit, difficult to correct. Whoa your pup at the first indication of having scent and do not allow it to take even a step. If the pup advances, stop it without negativity, pick it up, and return it to the point of original scent. After you have whoaed the pup at the site of original scent, if the bird still has not flown, it can be flushed and shot. Whoaing after taking a step or two is not acceptable behavior; it will lead to creeping and disaster on wild birds. Do not shoot bumped birds. Whoa means whoa, a lesson your pup already should have learned away from birds. If the bird is bumped, stop the pup with the check cord without being overly corrective or involving yourself in the stop. Once stopped, pick up the pup and return it to the original site. Keep the pup on whoa in a positive manner for a short time, then release it and take in the opposite direction from the bird's flight.

Also be ready if the bird decides not to fly or walk around in plain view of the pup. Again, using the check cord, whoa the pup while your helper flushes or runs the bird out of sight. Then release the pup and take it in the opposite direction from the bird. If you wish to use that bird again, hunt around for a while, then come in on it from another direction. Do this only if you think you can get the bird to fly.

Unusual bird behavior can be turned into a positive if you are ready and do the right thing. In the end, a staunch dog that will hold no matter what the bird does will be the result. Refining manners to this point is difficult when using only wild birds. Clients have been impressed on more than one occasion when one of my dogs held point while a bird ran back and forth within a few feet of the dog in plain view. The only reason for poor pointing manners is a lack of training and attention to detail by the handler.

When using a preserve to extend the season for your seasoned performer, ask to shoot scratch or have your birds free-released, not planted. Doing this along with shooting only points and having only one shooter on each point makes the experience more satisfying. Approach the preserve experience for what it is—a chance to extend your dog's season and refine its manners.

An anecdotal experience may best serve to show the potential of preserves. Tuck came to me at five months of age as a true providence, the result of an unexpected set of circumstances. He was well socialized but had no real training. Two months of work in the yard and on pen birds at my place had him ready for a controlled shoot on the preserve. At seven months, during the December break between the two grouse seasons in Pennsylvania, we took him on his first hunt. Four huns were released, and Mike Conner and I began our hunt. The end product was four productive points, four birds taken, and four retrieves. The event that shows the possibilities of preserves and demonstrated Tuck's potential involved a pair of huns that had taken refuge along a woods edge in some red briers. Tuck pointed and a pair of huns was sighted. I went in to flush with Mike at ready. Upon flushing, I picked out one bird and shot, seeing it fold just before Mike's twenty also barked once. Mike began to apologize as Tuck

My dog Tuck pointing a training bird at one year.

went for the retrieve. Thinking he had shot at the second bird, I was slightly confused. Mike explained that the second bird had not flushed and that he had unavoidably shot at the same bird an instant after I had shot. About that time, Tuck swung by the briers, carrying the dead bird softly in his mouth. He wheeled and pointed the second bird while still holding the first in his mouth. I flushed the second bird and watched as Mike missed, marking it down in the adjacent field. Tuck watched also, then nonchalantly turned and completed the retrieve to hand. Mike's comment was simply "How old did you say that dog is?"

One preserve outing of an hour or so had given Tuck more bird experience than a month's wild bird hunting could have provided in our area of the country. Additionally, there was almost zero potential for problems. As a well-started dog at one and a half years, Tuck would later prove himself in grouse woods.

Don't scoff at preserves. If a lack of birds is a problem for you and your dog, give them a chance. Preserve birds are better than no birds, and handling the situation correctly will negate potential problems. The quality of the experience will depend on the quality of the preserve and how you approach the situation. As with other training, success depends on the two-legged member of the canine-human partnership.

CHAPTER SEVEN

Beyond the First Season

If puppy training and the first season have gone well, between the first and second seasons you need to finish what you have begun and correct any problems that have arisen. Fine-tune your lessons and techniques to meet the needs of your dog at this point in its career. It takes at least two full seasons of hunting and training and the maturity that comes with age and experience to finish a pointing dog in the field.

STEADINESS TO WING AND SHOT

In the area of pointing manners, there is a good deal of variance in training from one handler to the next. As with all training, I feel it is best to finish your dog so that you have the necessary tools in place if problems arise later. Once steadied to wing and shot, a dog can always be allowed to slacken its pointing manners. But if you do not steady the dog and problems arise, you will have no recourse. I steady my setters to wing and shot at this point in their training, then, depending on the individual's propensity to chase, adapt each one's manners as needed in the field. In grouse woods, we eventually achieve what I call a modified steadiness. At the very least, your dog should be steady to wing for the sake of safety, learning to break only on shot.

The arguments against steadiness are far outweighed by the arguments in favor of it. The argument most often heard against steadiness is "I want my dog out there under a crippled bird so that it does not get away." In fact, my experience over thirty-five years with gun dogs has been that the opposite is true. A steady dog is more likely to have a good mark, being riveted on the bird's flight and seeing it crumple. A dog that is allowed to break and chase on flush is more likely to overrun the bird or be left or right of its flight path. A dog that is at least steady to wing will break on shot and still be on the scene in plenty of time. Often failure to steady a dog is simply the product of laziness or a lack of know-how.

Three-year-old Honey, staunch and steady on a training bird.

Thunder, a German shorthair male, steady to wing and shot at two years.

Arguments for steadiness are much more compelling. First, it is an issue of safety. A dog chasing a low-flying bird is a recipe for disaster, whereas a steady dog is out of harm's way. Second, a steady dog will not be as likely to wildly flush other birds that may be in front of you. Third, you are in control of the situation, not the dog. One of the basic rules is that the dog does not decide what behaviors are appropriate, you do. Finally, steadiness facilitates other training, such as stopping to flush and backing.

To achieve steadiness to wing or wing and shot, your dog needs to be mature enough and have had sufficient bird experience to properly respond to the pressure you are going to put on it. This is why you wait until after the pup's first season to take this training step. To steady the dog, you need to go back to the short check cord or the e-collar, if pup has been well conditioned to it during other training. Do not use the e-collar for the first time on birds. Using an e-collar for bird work is probably best left to a pro. Start with a positive approach to steadiness. When your dog points, use the check cord to get to it, and physically handle it on point. Hook a finger under its collar and slip your other arm under its belly. While you are handling the dog, have your assistant flush and shoot the bird. Handle and stroke the dog until it goes firm, then praise it and send it to retrieve.

Repeat the same technique while tossing the bird and firing the blank gun. Allow your dog to go for the retrieve only on your command. Use this technique until you think your dog understands the concept. Next, pick up the check cord when your dog points, and be ready when your assistant flushes and shoots the bird. Sensing freedom, your dog will probably break. Plant both feet and use the check cord to jolt it to a stop, saying nothing. Lift the dog up with one hand under the abdomen and the other under the neck. Carry it back to the site of the original point, place it down, and reestablish the pointing stance. Stroke until the dog goes firm, then release it to retrieve.

Switch back and forth from not shooting the bird to shooting it. Often it is best to achieve steadiness to the blank gun first before actually shooting the bird. If you do this, be prepared as before. When your dog sees the bird fall, it will break at first. Continue to go back and forth from positive handling to negative reinforcement with the check cord and from the blank gun to shooting the bird. A physical touch on the head when releasing the dog with "okay" will help steady it. If the dog learns to wait for that tap on the head, it will be less likely to jump the gun.

Continue to steady in the yard with a winged dummy and blank gun. Stand on the check cord behind the pup while tossing the dummy and firing the blank gun. If the dog breaks, allow the check cord to jolt it to a stop, saying nothing. Pick the dog up and place it back on the original site of your "stay" ("whoa") command. Stroke until the dog stands on its own, then release it with "okay" and the head tap, sending it to complete the retrieve. I like to do this exercise immediately before going into the field for steadiness training on real birds. Here again, repetition is the key.

While steadying to wing and shot, I like to do a lot of stopping to flush and backing. All three of these are teaching your dog the same lesson: to stay (whoa) any time it scents or sees a bird. Stopping to flush and backing manners are not related to bird scent, so the pressure being put on the dog is not related to bird scent either. In a sensitive dog, I may achieve stopping to flush and backing manners before introducing steadiness on scent points.

When your dog will stand through the shot and kill, not moving until you release it to retrieve, you have a steady dog. Do not be surprised if during the second season, it starts to break down some. The dog will sense that your attention is not entirely on it as in training, and sensing freedom, it will start to move on flush. Keeping your dog steady under actual hunting situations is an ongoing chore. This is when you can decide if it is worth it or if you will only enforce steadiness to wing, allowing the dog to break on shot. A gun dog that is steady to wing only is practical yet safe. Dogs that will be hunting quail or other covey birds should be kept steady to both wing and shot.

STOPPING TO FLUSH

Stopping to flush means that your dog stops and assumes the pointing stance when it accidentally bumps a bird or a bird gets up for some other reason. Upon hearing or seeing the bird, the dog should stay (whoa) and hold the pointing stance until released. This serves the same purpose as steadiness to wing and shot on a scented bird. In addition, once the dog is well advanced, this allows the hunter to shoot the bird, since the dog has displayed proper manners. You can teach this response with or without remote flushing pens. I prefer pigeons for this exercise, because they will not fly to the ground when released. Carry birds on you while the dog quarters in front of you dragging the check cord. Call the dog's name, and when it looks at you, hand-toss a bird and stay (whoa) the dog. If necessary, use the check cord to stay the dog. Once it begins to stay, add the blank gun to the equation. From here, use launchers if you have them. Put pigeons out in the launchers, and quarter the dog toward them upwind, as you do not want the dog to smell the birds. When the dog quarters past the bird at a short distance, launch the bird and stay (whoa) the dog. Again, use the check cord for any necessary correction. Once the dog stays on flush on its own, reintroduce the blank gun. Release with "okay" and a physical touch.

Stopping to flush will facilitate steadiness training and is both a practical and aesthetic addition to your dog's training.

BACKING OR HONORING

If you have hunted your youngster with another, older dog during its first season, it may have begun to back naturally. It is a natural tendency in many dogs. My experience has been that biddable dogs tend to do it more naturally. If so, you should be praising and reinforcing your dog for doing so. Use your "stay" ("whoa") command to reinforce, then praise. As I will illustrate, it also helps to allow the backing dog to retrieve as a reward. To

Old Hemlock Spirit pointing for owner Jeff Kauffman. JEFF KAUFFMAN

progress with this training, you need either a finished older dog or an artificial backing dog made of plywood and painted. You can purchase an electronic backing dog, but these are expensive and probably not worth it, except for the pro.

If your dog has not been hunted with other dogs or has not shown an instinct to back, now is the time to teach it. A dog that steals another's point is not appreciated in pointing-dog circles and will get you uninvited to the next hunt. Backing also has both practical and aesthetic reasons for being taught. First, the dog on scent point is often immersed in thick cover. The backing dog serves as a sign to the hunter that there is a point ahead. Second, backing allows the hunter to know which dog gets credit for the find. Third, stealing the point may cause the pointing dog to creep, resulting in a bumped bird. Fourth, it is the prettiest sight in the field to see two dogs locked in a point and back point.

When teaching with an artificial backing dog, place the artificial dog around a corner or over the crest of a hill so the approaching pupil will not see it until upon it. Put the bird ahead of the artificial, upwind from

English setter and pointer executing a point and backpoint. MARIO T. EUSI

the approaching pupil. When the pupil sees the artificial, stay (whoa) your dog and handle it in a positive manner. Have an assistant flush and shoot the bird. Steady the dog, then send it to retrieve. Lower the artificial while the pupil is on the way to retrieve. The first time you use one, it can also help to stay (whoa) the pupil, then pick up the pup and carry it past the artificial pointing dog until the pup smells the bird. Then take the pupil back to the original site and proceed as before. The combination of your stay (whoa) training, letting the dog retrieve, and natural instinct will help teach backing, along with repetition. If you are using a live dog instead of an artificial, the procedure is the same once the lead dog has established a scent point. Be sure this dog is well finished.

Steadiness, stopping to flush, and backing are all components of a finished dog. If your dog does not achieve these, it is not finished. The degree to which your dog is finished is up to you.

OTHER FINE-TUNING

The extent to which other lessons need to be continued after the first sea-son varies from dog to dog. You may need to refine coming or quartering using the same techniques or possibly introduce the e-collar, if your dog is a candidate. You may need to work on finishing retrieving technique. Training should continue but often is a matter of advancing lessons already learned to a higher level. Keep your dog in good shape during the off-season, adjusting its diet as needed and doing some cross-training, such as swimming. Be aware of legal training seasons in your state and watch the weather. In much of the country, preseason training is done in hot summer weather. Work your dog in the early-morning hours until the weather begins to cool.

The advanced lessons taught between the first and second season will be tested during the second season. Keep working on them while hunting. Your dog is truly finished when it performs all of these tasks properly under real hunting conditions.

Rose and me on our trek back to the truck after a successful hunt.
JEFF KAUFFMAN

CHAPTER EIGHT

Problems, Problems, Problems

In thirty-five years, it has been my pleasure to own a couple of dogs that progressed through their training with no real problems. But most have had a few minor problems that took minimal correction. I have avoided major problems with good breeding, preventive training, and very biddable dogs. I see real problems all the time in clients' dogs, however. Usually they are the result of the wrong breeding, a lack of early training, or both. I hope this book will help you avoid real problems. This chapter is aimed at curing a few of the more common ones.

First you must decide if the behavior in question is really a problem or just an idiosyncrasy that you can live with. Do not develop tunnel vision in handling your pup. There are many ways to get the end result of an effective partnership with your gun dog. Emphasize your pup's strengths and work around its weaknesses. I start with the same training guidelines for all my pups, but each proceeds in a unique manner and pace. Each pup's personality is allowed to blossom during training and shows in the finished product. Individualized training unfolds as I get to know each pup, and it becomes the focal point of each relationship.

If your dog does develop a real problem that interferes with your ability to function as partners in the field or at home, it needs to be corrected. In many cases, this may require the services of a professional trainer. If you decide to correct the problem yourself, you must first decide what caused the problem. Knowing the cause will help you develop corrective action. Proceed carefully, getting professional advice as needed.

Some problems are more easily dealt with than others. This chapter deals with a few of the major gun-dog problems. In discussing each problem, I will first review preventive training techniques discussed earlier, then discuss the cure. The preventive training techniques are often at the heart of corrective training.

Male pointer focused on bird. MARIO T. EUSI

DEER CHASING

There are some undesirable habits in gun dogs that can be tolerated; scent-tracking deer is not one of them. Like most bad habits, it can be avoided with proper attention to detail and keen dedication during early training. Unfortunately, many owners seem to be as crisis-oriented as the rest of our society. They do not worry about a behavioral problem until it has already developed, then express amazement at its presence. Many may have believed that buying a high-priced pup and allowing nature to take its course was all that was needed. Or they waited until the pup was too old to seek training for it. It's important to outline and undertake a training regimen that will prevent deer chasing and other bad habits before they begin. In the long run, prevention is easier and cheaper than the cure.

Deer chasing can lead to the loss of a pup, the loss of the owner's sanity, or both. Dogs are innate hunters, but we must teach them what to hunt and what not to hunt. Ground-tracking breeds are more prone to deer chasing than air-scenting ones, although it can become a problem in any dog if early training is not thoroughly done.

Let's first review the early training steps that can help prevent deer chasing before undertaking the cure. First, develop positive dog-human rapport at an early age. A gun dog that has a genuine bond with its partner will be more likely to hunt for the gun and less likely to do its own thing. Its primary goal will be to please you, and it will avoid things that do not. A pup with this kind of demeanor will be less likely to wander in the field. To develop this kind of relationship, you must become the center of your pup's world. Feed, clean, groom, and train the pup yourself. Good rapport is the basis of everything you do with your youngster. Second, thoroughly obedience train your pup. Start young, and progress with daily sessions as described in this text. Regular sessions of serious training will instill the necessary control. You command and your pup obeys. Once total obedience is achieved in the yard, be sure to do your transition training to the field by gradually introducing distractions and using negative reinforcement when necessary. You want to be able to control your pup under any and all circumstances. How does this help prevent deer chasing? It gives you the needed control to keep your pup close and out of trouble during its first season. Also, it enables you to stop a sight chase or discipline if one develops. Deer chasing often starts when an out-of-control pup is away from its handler and, sensing freedom, begins to investigate other sights and scents. Third, make sure your pup is very birdy before going into situations where there are deer. Exposing it to dozens, even hundreds, of training birds will have the pup hunting with intensity and purpose and will help override interest in other scents. The more the pup's mind is on bird scent, the less likely it will get involved with something else. If it does, you can discipline accordingly, because the pup knows why it is out there. Fourth, select your covers carefully during the first season, and don't get greedy about killing large numbers of wild birds. Numbers can be achieved with training birds and shooting preserves. Try to stack the deck toward successful outings during the first season. Be willing to sacrifice some hunting. Plan your strategy and hunt in a manner that has your pup's best interests in mind. Picking small, familiar covers where your pup is less likely to wander will be a plus.

In general, the first season with a pup should be dedicated to getting it started in the right direction and not allowing problems to develop. If you are not willing to do this, a started or finished dog would be a better investment. Too many potentially good gun dogs are ruined by overly zealous owners intent on killing large numbers of birds and ignoring their pups' welfare. That many pups survive this kind of handling is a tribute to their breeding. Nevertheless, an ounce of prevention is worth a pound of cure. If your dog does develop a deer-chasing problem during its first season, do not allow it to continue. The more engrained this becomes, the more difficult it is to cure. Stop hunting the pup and get to the task at hand, breaking the deer chasing. Be sure of your diagnosis and proceed with caution. You can usually tell the difference between a dog that is trailing deer versus other scent: It will drop its nose and take off in a straight line, not to return for minutes, hours, maybe even days. I am not talking about a short sight chase that you can correct with immediate discipline, but a dog that drops its nose and takes off every time it crosses a deer trail. If you are not sure, set up a situation by leading your pup across a trail where you have seen deer in the past few minutes and watch its reaction. Once engrained, this behavior will ruin every hunt and put your pup's life in danger.

There are numerous old remedies for this problem. Most are tricky to carry out and only partly successful at best. Deer chasing is one problem

German shorthair female steady to wing and shot at three years.
DONNIE EBERSOLE

best dealt with by corrective use of the e-collar. If you are not confident of your ability to do this, seek out a pro that uses the e-collar for this purpose. The e-collar is quick and far more effective than any other technique I have seen used for this purpose. It has never failed to work for me with clients' dogs of various types and breeds.

If you choose to attempt the task on your own, follow the procedure outlined here. Find a place where you can see deer out in the open, and park your vehicle within a few hundred yards or closer. Open fields, power lines, golf courses, and ski slopes are all likely places. Keep the dog in the vehicle with the e-collar on and active until you see deer, then lead your pup on a check cord to the area where you saw them. The pup should not see the deer, which will probably vacate the area before that might happen anyway. Turn the pup loose when you arrive at the area where the scent trails have been left. When the pup puts its nose down and takes off on scent, use a high level of stimulation to stop the behavior. This is what the higher levels on the collar are designed for. It should be an unpleasant experience for the pup. When the pup stops the behavior, call it to you and lead it from the area. You may come back to the same area five or ten minutes later and use the same procedure a second time, if the pup again shows interest in the scent. When the pup starts to scent trail, allow enough time to be sure of the behavior, but do not allow the pup to get too far away. Any misbehavior is more easily corrected if you apply the correction early in the misdoing. Use this same technique another session or two, until the pup shows no interest in the scent. Once compliance is achieved in the setup situation, take the pup on a mock hunt where you know you will encounter deer. If the pup engages in scent-tracking, correct the behavior immediately, using a high level of correction.

While the process is under way, do not hunt the pup. The behavior should be corrected before the pup is put into a real hunting situation. The training should be concentrated in a short period of time so that the pup has good recall of the previous session. Once the behavior is corrected, resume hunting with the dog wearing either a live or a dummy collar. If the behavior recurs, go back to corrective measures. Usually a reminder while hunting suffices once the initial lesson has been learned.

In summary, deer chasing can usually be prevented with proper early training. If you do need to correct chasing, the experience will not be a pleasant one for your pup, but do not hesitate to use enough pressure to get the job done. You may be saving your dog's life.

BLINKING, OR BIRD SHYNESS
Blinking is often a misunderstood and misdiagnosed problem acquired by gun dogs of all types. It is most often associated with the pointing breeds, for reasons inherent in its cause. A novice handler might well confuse it with gun shyness, a lack of pointing instinct, or a poor-quality nose. In fact, the dog smells the bird, but because of unpleasantness associated with bird scent, it makes an attempt to avoid the bird once encountered. A blinker may hunt with intensity, evidence of its innate drive, but displays an avoidance technique when encountering scent. Gun shyness may be a companion trait to blinking, but true blinking is a problem with causative factors of its own.

Depending on the degree of the problem, a dog may point, then slink away from the bird, or it may avoid the bird altogether once it identifies the scent. What has happened to your young prospect that showed so much enthusiasm on its first ventures afield? What did this youngster experience that was so frightening as to override its innate pointing instinct? To your pup and to you, this can be a perplexing problem.

First, understand that although this is not an innate problem, particularly sensitive pups are more prone to it. Some pups can become blinkers as a result of training techniques that work fine for others. Simply, blinking is the result of too much pressure associated with birds and bird scent being put on the pup too soon. If a pup associates harsh handling with bird scent, it will do the sensible thing and avoid it. Do not handle your pup on birds before it is ready, and do not try to force the pup to point. Do not check cord your pup into a planted bird and stay (whoa) it on its first outings. Your pup should be allowed to find, flush, and chase birds, developing the pointing instinct naturally and building enthusiasm for bird scent. Some pups will gain boldness and show point earlier than others; some will show point on their first trip afield. Often the more biddable pups will show point sooner yet take longer to build the drive necessary for handling and staunching them on point.

Use good judgment, giving your pup sufficient time to get fired up about birds. At the same time, you should be well along with your stay (whoa) training in the yard and other situations away from birds. Your pup should be confident with the command long before it is used in connection with birds. When your pup is showing sufficient boldness and pointing instinct, you can start to verbally stay (whoa) it when approaching to flush the bird. Early bird contacts should be fun, reinforcing your pup's natural drive. If you allow sufficient time and birds before starting to staunch your pup, it will develop sufficient boldness to handle training. I have seen blinkers made that way by pros that did not know they had done anything wrong. Know your pup's temperament and proceed accordingly.

The cure for blinking is the same as the prevention, only more of it—much more. It may take hundreds of birds to cure blinking. In addition, you may have to allow all of the pup's training to break down, encouraging its natural instincts back to the surface. The time and cost involved in curing blinking should be enough to cause you to want to prevent it, slowing down and giving your pup time to develop its bird instincts before putting any pressure at all on it. Simply diagnosing blinking may require a professional opinion, and a pro may be the only one with the resources to cure it. At this point, you may have to make some tough decisions. Is the pup worth the hundreds of dollars it may take to cure the problem? The extent and degree of the problem also need to be diagnosed before making a final decision. I have seen dogs that would blink on planted birds but point wild or liberated ones staunchly. Some dogs may even identify certain bird species as the source of their problem, yet point others staunchly. Potential reasons for these behaviors are the human scent on planted birds and the harsh handling associated with the bird species used in training. Wild or liberated birds should be used to introduce pups to birds or cure the older confirmed blinker.

Some handlers have a specific training regimen that they apply to all pups. If a pup breaks down under the pressure, it goes back to the owner with the excuse that it just did not have it. This philosophy is unfair, untrue, and perhaps inhumane. I have seen many pups that were late to develop become outstanding gun dogs. In fact, often the more sensitive and intelligent pups are the ones that notice unnatural conditions the most. Follow the procedures outlined earlier in the text, let your pup have fun, and do not push it too hard, too soon.

If your pup has become a blinker and you have decided it is worth the cure, proceed with caution. You must go back to the beginning. Use wild or liberated birds, no human scent, and no artificial conditions. Do no handling; you are along only for the walk, and your pup is allowed to do whatever it wants. Do not react to whatever your pup does in any way; simply observe. There must be gobs of bird scent and no interference. Be patient. This will take ten times the birds and time than it would have taken to do it right to begin with. You should also back off other training during this time. Do nothing to put any pressure on the pup. You are gambling that the pup's latent instinct will surface, and if it does, let it build without interference. With luck, your pup will start to chase birds and even catch one. You are encouraging the opposite of what would be normal progression at this time. You are going back to the beginning. If your pup starts to show point, say and do nothing at first. Allow it to flush and chase. If the points become more staunch on their own, simply walk in and flush the bird. Again, say and do nothing else. If this progression continues for weeks, even months, with the pup getting bolder, kill a bird for it. Again, say or do nothing except shoot the bird. If the pup brings you the bird, accept it and praise profusely. If not, fine. Pick up the bird where the pup leaves it and continue on.

This process can be painstakingly slow and tedious, but you have no choice except to go slow. Continue to train and hunt with no handling. Everything has to happen naturally, from finding to pointing to shooting the birds. You are sacrificing manners to build drive and enthusiasm. You may never be able to finish this pup. Staunchness may have to be the ultimate goal. If you can achieve it, you have beaten the odds.

The nature and degree of the problem will determine whether you can cure it. True blinkers on all species of birds, in all situations, are rarely cured completely. A situation- or species-specific blinker is more easily dealt with and has a greater chance to be cured. A dog that shows no point at all and exhibits total avoidance will be more difficult to cure than one that points and holds for a while before backing off. As you can see, the correctness of the diagnosis has much to do with the likelihood of a cure. You should consult a competent pro, skilled in handling blinkers, who will be familiar with and equipped to undertake more creative and radical techniques. If you choose to try to cure a blinker yourself, pray that your dog's instincts are strong enough to override a human-created condition.

GUN SHYNESS

Like blinking, gun shyness is a created condition. There is no such thing as an innately gun-shy dog. Sensitive pups are more prone to develop it, but it is the result of careless or overzealous handling. Once the affliction is engrained, it will take many birds, much patience, and a skilled handler to cure. The one advantage is that the pup's bird drive can be used to help override it, an advantage that does not exist in the case of blinking. Again, the real shame is that it could have been avoided with proper and careful introduction of the gun. Even the most sensitive pup will come to love the gun when properly introduced in association with birds.

Obviously, choosing a pup from a solid gun-dog bloodline with a reputation for sound temperaments is a good first step. Next, be careful to develop a positive, trusting relationship with your pup. Such a relationship will help foster a bold pup, unafraid of new experiences. Start your pup on fun walks for birds only when it is physically and emotionally ready. Allow it to find birds, build confidence in new surroundings, and start to introduce the gun only when the pup is excited about birds. My setters are late to mature emotionally. Take your pup's temperament into account when progressing with the gun. Proceed only when the pup has become mature enough to accept this important new step. At this time, the pup should be comfortable with other loud noises, well along in obedience training, and eager to accept new experiences. Make sure it has frequent

Male setter retrieving to owner at one year. ROBERT WARNER

bird contacts. When the pup is eagerly flushing and chasing birds, you can slowly introduce crimp blanks at a distance. I use .22 crimp blanks at first. Never use live rimfire loads around pups. The shrill crack is harder on their hearing than a shotgun blast. Also, be careful with random shooting around the kennel before the pup is sufficiently broken to the gun.

Proceed with the gun as described in chapter 4 and continue carefully through the first season as set forth in chapter 5. As with other problems, prevention is easier and cheaper than the cure. Also, it is always easier to deal with a problem if it is correctly identified early. Hunters who are more interested in killing birds than they are in their pup's development will often be at fault in the onset of gun shyness. The philosophy and treatment for curing gun shyness is the same as the prevention, only with more birds. A dog's bird drive holds the key to both preventing and curing the problem.

If the pup seems to be overreacting to the gun, put it away. Do not try to force the gun on your pup. Just as throwing a pup out of a boat in the middle of a lake is more likely to make it afraid of water than teach it to swim, blasting away over your pup's head for no reason is likely to make it gun shy. Unlike the cure for blinking, you do not have to allow other training to break down. Just put the gun away and get the pup into more birds. You need to encourage a bird-crazy attitude. This will take many birds and much time. Follow the same procedures as when you first started on birds, but with no gun. Continue the bird work until the pup is fanatical about birds and bird scent. This may take weeks, even months, of bird work. When you think your pup is ready and is on a bird, start with .22 crimp blanks at a distance of twenty yards or more in the middle of a chase. Hold the gun behind your back and muffle it with a gloved hand. If the pup still overreacts, go back to more bird work before trying again. If the pup reacts normally, proceed in baby steps, firing the gun a little closer from time to time. Do not use the gun every time, and when you do, continue walking as if you heard nothing. Your reaction or lack of it will lead by example. If you leave your emotional base, your pup will notice and worry.

Once you are able to shoot the crimp blanks over an actual point at the moment of the flush, you are ready to kill a bird. Use a light-gauge shotgun, and do not miss. Lavishly praise your pup over any effort at retrieving. Your pup's bird interest is your trump card in curing gun shyness. With dogs recovering from gun shyness, you must shoot only points for the entire season. Random flushes are not an option. Complete recovery will take a season or more, depending on the number of birds you are able to kill for your dog.

Another tip for how to avoid this problem also helps prevent creeping. When your dog is on point, do not sneak up from behind and pass directly beside it. Instead, circle out and come in at a right angle or toward the dog, where you are in its view. Do so briskly, getting the bird in the air with some dispatch. The dog will see you, the bird, and the gun all together and not be as alarmed as it would be at an unexpected shot from behind, over its head. Getting the bird into the air quickly also helps excite and reassure the dog. This approach may also help trap running birds.

Remember, both the prevention and the cure for gun shyness is birds, birds, birds, and more birds before introducing the gun. Then associate the gun with the bird in a positive manner.

RETRIEVING PROBLEMS

Retrieving is a secondary instinct in pointing dogs; the search instinct is much stronger. Also, much of what is done in staunching a dog is contrary to retrieving. Still, pointing dogs with the right breeding will retrieve naturally with a little encouragement at the right times in their development. The act of picking up and carrying objects is all you are looking for in your pup. In the wild, the next step would be to eat or bury what it is carrying. Your job is to stop those behaviors short and teach your pup to bring the object to you. Many of the modern competitively bred pointing dogs have lost this instinct. It is not encouraged or desired in most field trials. Breeders of these dogs ignore it, and over time it is lost. This is particularly true among setters and pointers. If your pup shows no instinct to pick up and carry, you may have to settle for pointing dead or force-break your pup at a later time. I have never owned a dual-type setter that was not a strong natural retriever, and I refine it with repeated lessons as an integral part of its training. I favor dogs that hunt to the gun, point early, and retrieve naturally. I do not force-break my pups and send customers elsewhere to have it done.

Like children, pups have readiness stages for learning certain lessons. The instinct to chase a thrown object, pick it up, and carry it usually surfaces early. When it does, use the techniques outlined in earlier chapters to encourage and refine it. You do not want to destroy the instinct by applying too much discipline at an early age. Build excitement and lavish praise every time the pup brings an object to you. Staying (whoaing) on the toss, hunting dead, and sitting to deliver can all come later. Unlike obedience training, retrieving should be a fun game early in your pup's life. Once it is well engrained, you can teach your pup the appropriate manners involved. Most problems develop as a result of too much pressure too early in the process. Use every opportunity outside of training sessions to encourage the retrieving instinct. Never discipline your pup for picking up and carrying objects around the house or yard. Call it to you,

Brandi, a Brittany female, with a large Pennsylvania cock grouse.

command "drop," and accept the object with praise. You must differentiate between chewing and simply picking up and carrying. The more engrained the "fetch," "come," and "drop" commands are, the more likely they will work when starting to kill birds in the field. If your pup does not catch on right away in the field, use the transition techniques discussed in early chapters.

Here are the keys to prevent retrieving problems: Make early retrieving fun; do not use too much discipline too early in the process; never approach the pup in a threatening manner while it is in the act of retrieving, and use the proper techniques to get the pup to you; and never grab the dummy away from the pup as soon as it gets to you. Allow it to sit, hold the dummy, and receive praise until it is ready to drop the object. If you approach this correctly and the pup has sufficient instinct, it will be retrieving birds sometime during its first season.

Retrieving problems involve not picking up at all, short stopping and dropping the bird, and less commonly, hardmouth. Not picking up may be a lack of instinct or a fear of doing something wrong instilled by mishandling. If the pup never showed an instinct to pick up, this is probably a result of its breeding and will require force-breaking. If it showed an instinct to pick up but then stopped, something happened to turn the pup off to retrieving. It may be just a lack of understanding of what you expect. Moments earlier, you were staunching the pup on point and impressing on it not to grab the bird; now you are asking it to do the opposite. If this is the case, go to the transition techniques discussed earlier.

If the pup is fussing over a shot bird, pick it up and toss it for the pup, more closely replicating the yard work you have done. If this does not work, go back to the yard and work on retrieving, changing only one thing at a time until you get to a shot bird. First, put wings on the dummy but change nothing else from your previous sessions. Once the pup is retrieving the winged dummy with confidence, put the gun into the equation, again changing only one thing. From here go into the field with the winged dummy. If this goes well, use a dead bird, tossing it like the dummy. Next, try shooting over the pup again. You are filling in the gap between a dummy in the yard and a shot bird, one step at a time. If the pup was retrieving the dummy reliably before you started field training, this will work. If you did not do early dummy work, you have no tools to work with.

Another technique for addressing this problem involves allowing the pup to chase and catch wing-clipped or flagged pigeons. Fire the blank gun and toss the pigeon. The erratic flopping around should entice the pup to chase and grab the bird.

Short stopping—when a pup gets the bird or dummy but only brings it partway to the owner before dropping it—is usually the result of too much pressure being put on the pup during early training or dead bird work in the field. Use your come whistle so the pup does not misinterpret voice inflections, which are natural in the excitement of the moment. Turn and move hurriedly away while blowing the come whistle. You have presented the pup with a positive dilemma. It has this bird that it wants, and you are leaving. This works nine out of ten times. When the pup does get to you with the dummy or bird, do not grab it away immediately. Grasp the pup's collar, sweet talk, and praise. The most vital part of the entire process is to impress on the pup just how great it is for bringing you the dummy or bird. Be patient, do not approach, and do not rush out to the bird, doing the pup's job for it. If you retrieve, the pup figures it is not supposed to. Stay on your normal emotional plateau. Overly zealous behavior will make the pup worry whether it is anger or excitement. Again, you can go back to the yard if you did the proper elementary work. Using the grooming table, you can teach the pup to take and hold the dummy on command and to drop on command. On the ground, you can use a check cord to ensure completion of the retrieve. The pup simply needs reassurance that bringing things to you is well received by you.

Hardmouth is a much more perplexing retrieving problem, but fortunately it is not that common. First, be sure what you are seeing is hardmouth. A young dog typically will do a lot of excited mouthing, with feathers flying and so on. Do not mistake this for hardmouth and discipline a youngster, ruining it for retrieving. Also, a crippled bird, especially a ringneck, may take some subduing. A hardmouthed dog will crack bones and tear a bird apart in a deliberate act of destruction. This behavior may be a result of a naturally destructive temperament or mishandling during the training process. Competing with your pup for the bird, pulling it out of the pup's mouth too hurriedly, or putting too much pressure on the pup may all be sources of this behavior. A bird that has been crunched by the shooter and is a mass of flesh and blood may also encourage chewing. If the behavior is situation-specific, it will probably not become a problem. Consider the circumstances, and be certain what you are seeing is true hardmouth.

Here again, it may take the services of a pro to diagnose and treat the problem. There are some techniques to help with hardmouth, but this may be one case where force-breaking is the only real answer. If caught in the early stages, you may cure it using bird harnesses, spiked birds, birds wrapped in wire, or frozen birds. If the problem has been allowed to advance too far, these probably will not be enough. It is best not to breed a dog that has a natural tendency toward this behavior. In fact, many problems can be avoided by breeding natural gun dogs, not ones that have been forced into being top performers.

OTHER PROBLEMS

Other problems involving range, handling, bird manners, and more can arise during the first season. Address these things as soon as they are apparent, and give your dog a chance to succeed before giving up on it. It takes breeding, training, and birds to develop a gun dog. Often more birds and more training are all that is needed. Just like people, some dogs are more natural than others. The ones that are not as natural may turn out to be satisfactory performers with time and patience, but do not breed them.

I recommend seeking a pro to help with any problem. In all likelihood, something in your training approach has caused these problems. A pro will be more emotionally removed and experienced in diagnosing and treating the problem and will also have the resources to deal with it.

CHAPTER NINE

Gun-Dog Nutrition

A seven-week-old gun-dog prospect costs $400 to $1,000. In addition, there are vet bills, training expenses, kennel facilities, dog crate for house, dog crate for transport, collars, leads, and much more. In all, a one-year-old gun-dog prospect will have cost you $1,500 or more. Or you could buy a one-year-old started dog for about that same amount.

Anyone who seriously pursues upland game or waterfowl with a gun dog has incurred all or most of these costs. Yet when it comes to nutrition, one of the most important aspects of a dog's health and welfare, saving a few dollars often takes precedence beyond reason. In fact, not only do discount and grocery store foods have the potential to harm your star prospect, but in the long run they are not a financial savings, even if the per-bag cost is less.

When your pup is seven weeks old, it should already be on a diet of high-quality puppy chow straight from the bag. When choosing puppy food, consider the eventual weight of your pup as an adult dog. Breeds and individuals that will be more than fifty pounds at maturity need special consideration. In general, puppies need more calories than adults; however, too many calories in a large-breed individual can cause bone-growth problems, just as too few calories can. If you have a large-breed pup, you should feed it a large-breed puppy formula or half puppy chow and half adult formula. Consult your vet or a qualified dog professional, and keep a close watch on your puppy's growth and development.

Feed twice a day from seven weeks until six months to a year, depending on the breed and individual. Condition your pup to be an eager eater by placing the food down at the same time every day and taking it away after twenty minutes or so. Your pup will soon learn to eat when food is placed down. A conditioned eater will be a joy to live with and a healthier individual. Spoiled dogs that pick at their food are often the result of improper feeding technique. Overfeeding, having food down

Six-week-old Honey playing ball.

all the time, and giving too many treats can all lead to problems. In a house dog, conditioned eating will also make bathroom habits more regular and predictable.

How do the nutritional demands of gun dogs differ from those of other dogs, and what factors should influence your choice of dog food? A dog's nutritional needs are based on many considerations—age, size, metabolism, and level of activity, to name a few. Puppies demand more and different-octane food than adults. Some smaller adult dogs may have greater needs than their larger counterparts because of metabolism alone. In general, working dogs—including herd dogs, sled dogs, and our gun dogs—have greater nutritional needs than nonworking breeds.

With gun dogs, we need to consider their metabolism, level of activity, whether they are housed outside or inside, and the time of year, striking a balance between all of these things. During the off- season, protein level percentages in the mid-twenties and fat levels from twelve to fifteen percent would suffice for most pointing dog adults. A month to a month and half before the season, the fat content should be raised to about 20 percent, depending on the individual and how hard it is being worked. A gun dog that is kept outside may double or even triple its caloric needs during the time when cold weather and hunting season coincide. The dog draws on stored fat both to perform and to resist cold temperatures. Protein levels should not be increased beyond the mid to upper twenty-some percent level under any but extraordinary circumstances.

More important than protein and fat levels is the quality of the ingredients the manufacturer uses. A high level of digestibility is achieved with high-quality ingredients, meaning more is used by the dog's system and there is less waste. A good-quality food should have a digestibility rate above eighty-five percent. Large amounts of poorly formed stool in an otherwise healthy dog may indicate poor-quality food or overfeeding. Other indicators are coat and skin condition and stamina. The bulk amount you feed your dog depends entirely on the digestibility rate of the food. Thus you will feed less of a higher-quality food, have a healthier dog, and not spend more money.

Not all protein, fat, or grain is of the same quality. Better-quality foods use ingredients that meet standards for consumption set by the Association of American Feed Control Officials (AAFCO), and many are graded fit for human consumption. Do these foods cost more? Not necessarily. The per-bag cost may be more, but because you give your dog less of these

Nena, a Brittany female pointing a training bird. MARIO T. EUSI

foods, the per-feeding cost may be the same or even less. You may be able to feed half as much with better results.

By law, the percentages of protein, fat, fiber, and other components are given on the bag, and the ingredients are listed in order by amount in the food. Suggested feeding amounts are also printed on the bag and are good starting points, though you should take into consideration the factors discussed above, adjust the amount to suit your dog, and do not allow it to get fat.

With regard to the actual ingredients, meat and fat for gun dogs should come from chicken unless there is an allergy or other problem. Chicken metabolizes into fatty acids and energy-producing enzymes more efficiently than other meat and fat sources. If your dog has a tendency to gain too much weight, you can try other, less-efficient sources of meat and fat. I also recommend that you avoid foods with artificial preservatives or soy. Quality foods can be purchased for reasonable prices. You need not buy one of the highest-priced brands to get quality. If you need advice, consult a series of professionals—trainers, breeders, and vets—making sure they understand your dog's needs and have no ties to a particular manufacturer.

Quality feeding will keep your dog healthier, performing at a higher level, and in the long run it will save you money.

CHAPTER TEN

Tools of the Trade

The phrase "it isn't rocket science" has been uttered thousands of times by dog trainers, including this one. Yet the majority of gun dogs never become finished performers.

Three essential elements contribute toward building a finished gun dog: breeding, training, and birds. More often than not, one or more of these elements is missing. If we assume that the abundance of birds is a trainer's responsibility, then the three elements become two. In my experience, a lack of training and birds are usually the reasons for a poorly performing gun dog. Excuses abound, including a lack of time or knowledge to do the job correctly. If you cannot do it yourself, then hire a competent pro specializing in your type of hunting and breed of dog. If you want to do it yourself, start with one or more of the many good training books such as this one, and consult a pro for help when needed. Training books will instruct you as to how and when to teach the various steps in both obedience and field training. Be sure to purchase the correct books for your needs.

As a trainer of thirty-five years, I have read many books and articles and have written a few myself, but I have never seen a book that fully explored the tools of the trade. What follows is an attempt to educate the reader about the tools available and how they are used in training a pointing-dog prospect. Having the proper equipment and knowing how to use it will go a long way toward making you a better trainer. At the end is a brief discussion of remote training collars that should be enough to get you started with one, if it is needed.

CRATES, KENNELS, AND DRAWERS

The manner in which you house and transport your new pup is of utmost importance, both for proper care of the pup and as a training aid. If you intend to keep your pup in the house, make it a family member, and get the most out of your relationship, the first step to housebreaking is crate-breaking. Crate-breaking is also an important part of your pup's training,

A well-deserved nap for Misty and her grouse after a hard day.

teaching it that it has a place and giving it a sense of security that both physical and behavioral boundaries accomplish. Crate-breaking and choosing the appropriate crate were covered in chapter 3.

The best means for transporting your pup depends on the type of vehicle you will be driving. Regardless, your pup should always be secured in the vehicle just as a child would be. If you own a SUV, van, or wagon of some type, a standard Vari-Kennel type crate will suffice. It should be secured so that it does not slide, roll, or fly across the vehicle in an emergency. Placing it on top of a storage drawer provides you the added benefit of using space that would otherwise be wasted for the storage of gear and training supplies. More sturdy metal crates and drawer units of many types are available as well. If transporting more than one dog, I recommend two crates instead of one double crate. They give you far greater versatility. A seat-belt harness can be used for short trips around town or if you drive a sedan, but a crate provides more cleanliness for a day spent training or hunting.

It is preferable that you keep your companion gun dog in the house; otherwise it is not much of a companion. If for some good reason you cannot keep your pup in the house, or if you wish a part-time residence for your pup when you are not home, build a good kennel facility. Prefab chain-link panels are easily assembled, and a concrete floor with good drainage is the most easily cleaned. When considering kennel size, the type of dog is the main concern, but always increase size in one direction for exercise. Six by twelve feet is better than eight by ten, four by fourteen is better than six by twelve, and so on. Provide a house that is wide enough from side to side for the grown dog to sleep, but not so big that its body heat cannot keep the space warm. It is preferable that the dog not be able to stand upright, which would give it leverage to dig at the floor and walls. The door should be located on one end at the front, with a windbreak and second door inside. The house should be insulated and kept off the ground for greater warmth and preventing wear. A hinged top helps in cleaning and maintaining the inside. If you place the house outside of the run but firmly attached to it, the dog will be less likely to use it as a launching pad to escape and will not be able to chew and damage it externally. One of the newer resting pads made of canvas or other weather-resistant surface will give your pup a place to rest outdoors and help prevent sores from kennel rub.

Grouse, AyA, and Tuck at two years.

No matter how hard you hunt, ninety percent of your dog's life will be spent in the house or kennel. Other than house or kennel, no other housing accommodations are acceptable. Running loose is not an option, nor is a tie-out chain. A dog that is safe, secure, and content with its living quarters will be a better-adjusted citizen and a healthier one.

COLLARS, BELLS, LEADS, AND CHECK CORDS

A variety of collars will be needed for maintenance and training of your gun-dog prospect. As the puppy will grow rapidly, it is best to purchase an adjustable collar, usually available in nylon with plastic snap buckles, to see your pup through the early months. Sturdier models will be needed later, as plastic buckles break apart under stress and nylon fades and frays with time. For field work, I prefer a fluorescent orange polyethylene-coated collar with a center ring instead of the standard D-ring. The poly coating is weather-resistant, and the center ring prevents snagging and is designed to roll off if the collar snags. The orange is a safety factor showing others that this is someone's gun dog and making the dog easier to locate in cover. Adding a bell to the collar allows you to keep track of your dog in heavy cover and also warns others that this is someone's valued

Shorthair male backing off-camera bracemate with style. DONNIE EBERSOLE

gun dog. Bells come in various shapes and sizes. I prefer one with a tone that carries but is not obnoxiously loud. The two I use most often are a medium-size Swiss bell and a brass tinkler. When I am working two dogs together, the different tones allow for instant identification.

For dress collars, I like rolled leather. My dogs have long hair, and their coats cover the rolled collars, allowing for an unbroken line. If your dog has short hair, a regular one-inch leather collar is attractive, sturdy, and practical. Choke collars may be necessary for teaching various commands, most notably "heel," but they are for training only and should never be left on the dog when not on a lead. I prefer standard chain chokers. Any reasonably tempered dog can be trained with one when properly attached and used. The end to which your lead is attached should come over the top of the dog's neck toward you and through the end ring, allowing it to cinch and relax as designed.

You will also need leads of various lengths and types. For early training, a standard six-foot lead is enough, and it can serve as your walking lead throughout the dog's life. Here again I prefer leather, but for training young pups, a fancy leather lead may not be the best choice. As training advances, you will need a twenty-, twenty-five-, or thirty-foot nylon or rope lead for obedience work, allowing you to get farther away while staying in control. It will also aid in teaching quartering and retrieving in the yard.

For field work, you will need both thirty- and seventy-foot check cords. The longer check cord is to teach quartering and to control chasing early in your pup's training. The shorter, thirty-foot lead is for the pup to drag freely once it is under control and pointing. You will pick it up when approaching the pup to work on pointing manners. You can save money by buying a one-hundred-foot clothesline. Cut the rope into seventy- and thirty-foot sections, attach a snap to one end of each, and tie a small knot in the other end to prevent fraying.

A lead and check cord are your umbilical cords to the pup. Through them, you transfer both the intent and tone of your commands. The check cord is the professional gun-dog trainer's most important tool until the pup is later put on a remote training collar, if that is done. A remote collar is nothing other than an invisible check cord.

Quartering on check cord at ten weeks.

WHISTLES AND LANYARDS

One of the most puzzling attitudes that I encounter in training clients is resistance to using a whistle. Perhaps it is from having seen misuse of the whistle or simply a lack of understanding. Whatever the reason, the novice owner needs to be educated about correct application and use of the whistle. My whistle commands as a pointing-dog person are confined to a single blast for "come" and two blasts for "this way" or quartering. I first teach these with verbal and hand signal commands, then convert to whistles by association.

Why use the whistle? The short answer is that it works, but the long answer is multifaceted. First, your pup will hear the verbal "come" and many other vocalized commands in the course of everyday life, when they may not be strictly enforced. Like children, they learn to tune you out much of the time. The whistle is used only in strict training, however, with the check cord or remote collar to enforce it every time. It becomes more meaningful, because failure to comply always brings swift correction and enforcement. Second, a whistle's tone carries better in the field and woods. Third, the whistle is less disruptive to game birds. Also, if you later use a remote collar, the dog will already be imprinted to the whistle, making the whistle even more effective. If you blow the whistle without enforcing it, it will become as ineffective as your voice, but if you use and enforce it properly, it works like magic.

Whistles come in many shapes, sizes, and tones. To train clients' dogs, I prefer a Fox 40. It carries well, and I like its pealess structure, which produces a single tone. For my own dogs, I use a hawk call, a trick I learned from the gentleman who taught me to grouse-hunt. Whatever whistle you choose, learn to use it correctly and sparingly.

Lanyards are not that complicated. They can be leather, nylon, or cotton and come in single-, double-, and multiple-whistle models. I use a double model to hold both a Fox 40 and my hawk call. Grouse hunters prefer ones that also have a flush counter and compass. Their simple purpose is to carry your whistles in a convenient and comfortable manner.

DUMMIES, DEAD FOWL, AND LAUNCHERS

I believe in breeding pups with a natural instinct to pick up and carry, then using the conditioned-retrieve method rather than force to turn them into reliable retrievers. In the pointing breeds, retrieving is a secondary instinct at best. Unfortunately, in breeding some of the modern competi-

English setter, Corey, retrieving dummy at five months.

tive bloodlines, this instinct has been ignored and lost altogether. Force-breaking has become the rage, but in my opinion, it is a poor substitute. Force-breaking leads to breeding dogs that lack instinct, which leads to more force-breaking, and so on.

In the pointing breeds, the approach to retrieving is different than in retrieving and flushing breeds. For these puppies, you need to start with a small, plain dummy with no scent. No scent or feathers should be involved until after the pointing dog is staunch and has had birds killed over it. A small canvas or plastic dummy or a tennis ball will suffice for puppy retrieving. Use larger dummies as the pup grows and matures. I like canvas, but many trainers prefer the plastic knobbies. Colors are usually white or orange. In cover, orange is more easily located by the trainer when necessary.

Once birds are killed and your dog is staunch on point, you can use dead-fowl dummies with scent and feathers, but only if your dog is whoaed and sent on a command to fetch. You can also use the blank gun in this exercise.

Remote launchers that are now used to launch birds were originally used to launch dummies, and you can employ them for that purpose later in the dog's development. Hand-held dummy launchers have become popular with retriever trainers but are not really needed with pointing dogs.

GLOVES AND BOOTS

I have had rope burns on my hands, wrists, arms, legs, and even neck from being on the opposite end of a check cord from a hard-charging pointing dog. A pair of leather gloves is a must for protection when using a check-cord in the field. Leather gloves also serve the purpose of reducing human scent when handling birds, launchers, or anything that is going to be part of the scent package for a young dog. Will they eliminate human scent? No, but they will noticeably reduce it. Sensitive breeds and individuals are particularly bothered by artificial conditions surrounding birds and pointing. Such artificiality could be part of a bigger set of conditions that might lead to creeping, softness on point, or even blinking. I like pliable deerskin gloves for hunting. After a season or two, they become training gloves and I buy a new pair for hunting.

In August, September, and early October, when I train in the early morning to avoid the heat, the grass is always wet. Wear an inexpensive pair of rubber boots to keep your feet dry. The constant soaking and drying will ruin leather boots. I don't hunt in rubber boots, but the morning training sessions do not involve vigorous or long-term walking like grouse hunting does.

BLANK GUNS AND LOADS

A blank gun is an essential piece of equipment for correctly introducing a young pup to gunfire. A .22-caliber one that shoots only crimp blanks is inexpensive and will last a season to two. Better ones can be purchased for $75 to $100. You can use your regular .22 pistol, but be sure to start with crimp blanks, not full load blanks. Also, never use live rimfire rounds near a pup. The shrill crack is more traumatic than a shotgun blast, and live rounds are not safe. I go from .22 crimp blanks to a shotgun, but if you wish, you can go from a .22 to a .32 crimp blank, then to a shotgun. If you use your regular pistol, be careful of muzzle blast, and clean the gun regularly. The black powder used in crimp blanks will foul your barrel.

More recently, blank guns that fire shotgun primers have become popular. If you reload for your shotgun, they may be more practical, as you will have them on hand. Most dog-supply catalogs offer crimp blanks, but the hazardous shipping fee is expensive. I use hundreds of crimp blanks each training season, so I buy them in bulk when they are locally available or to save on the shipping cost if ordering by mail.

ARTIFICIAL BACKING DOGS

Every well-mannered pointing dog should back or honor its bracemate. If you start this training early, it can be easily engrained. Whether you are reinforcing a pup's natural tendency or forcing it to back, an artificial backing dog is an essential tool.

The simplest one is a plywood silhouette painted to resemble a dog, with metal stakes on the feet to stick into the ground. Place it around a bend in the woods or over the crest of a hill, with a bird in a launcher or trap in front of the pointing silhouette, and work the pup upwind into a position where it will see the silhouette at a distance of ten yards or so. If the pup stops naturally, reinforce it with a positive "whoa," flush the bird, and praise. As an additional incentive to back, you can shoot the bird and allow the backing dog to retrieve. This is a sight-only exercise; no scent should be involved in the back. If the pup does not back naturally, use your "whoa" command and strictly enforce it. More repetition will be needed with a reluctant backer.

Remote-controlled backing dogs are much more versatile but very expensive. They are a worthwhile investment only for a pro or serious hobbyist. I use one but also have a stake-in silhouette as a backup in case the batteries go on the remote one.

Using a real dog as the lead is an option if you have a totally dependable veteran performer that is steady to wing, shot, and command. Using a real dog may necessitate an assistant to handle it and to shoot. I prefer to teach with the artificial dog first, then run a few sessions with a real dog once the lesson is well in place. The change to a real dog may require some reinforcement with your trainee. Also, most commercial silhouettes are white dogs with dark spots and tails. A brown dog with a docked tail presents a different picture and can confuse some youngsters. Take this into consideration and include a real dog in your training regimen if your pup will be hunting with a different breed from the one pictured on the backing silhouette.

BIRD LAUNCHERS, TRAPS, AND HARNESSES

There was a time when I did all of my training on wild birds, but that time is long gone. Now there aren't enough wild birds in our area of Pennsylvania even to start one pup. This necessitates pen birds, which in turn necessitates launchers, traps, and various other equipment to allow me to present birds to a pup in the most realistic and natural fashion.

I now start pups on "liberated" quail presented as naturally as possible. The pup's interest and drive build, and it soon starts to show point. Shortly, I get away from the quail for the same reason I use them in the beginning. They are low, short-flighted birds that encourage a pup to chase. When I want to work on pointing manners and end the chasing, I go to remote launchers with homing pigeons or chukar, depending on whether we are killing the bird or not. In my opinion, remote launchers are the single most important electronic innovation for dog training. They provide more scent than a planted bird and allow a natural approach, point, and flush. Because you have the transmitter in hand, you do not need to use a check cord or put pressure on the pup. If the pup points, approach and flush the bird just like a wild bird, fire the blank gun, and reward the dog. If the pup moves on the bird, launch it, providing the same natural correction a wild bird would provide, and do any postflush correction appropriate for the pup's age and level of training. Remote launchers are not cheap, but at least one company makes a model that is compatible with its training collar and transmitter. This lessens the expense and makes a convenient, versatile outfit.

You can purchase the same style launcher much more cheaply in a manual model equipped with a pull cord of any length desired. Bob Warner of www.bobwhitequail.com retrofits these launchers with step

Male English setter retrieving for owner. ROBERT WARNER

INDEX

ACKNOWLEDGMENTS

I would like to thank the following people: Dr. Howard Hoffman, who introduced me to grouse hunting and pointing dogs, then mentored me for years. George Bird Evans, whose *Upland Shooting Life* inspired me and whose guidance led me to my first dual-type English setter. Ken Alexander of DeCoverly Kennels, whose instruction in breeding, genetics, and dual-type English setters provided me with a wealth of information. David Michael Duffy, whose *Hunting Dog Know How* contributed invaluable training knowledge early in my career. Richard Wolters, whose *Gun Dog* helped me form my philosophy and positive-reinforcement approach to puppy training.

APPENDIX C

Canine First-Aid Kit

Electrolyte liquid, glucose tabs or powder (carry in vest)
Smelling salts (carry in vest)

Tweezers or hemostats (carry in vest)
Brewer's yeast tablets

Buffered aspirin
Cotton roll

Cut-heal ointment
Eyewash

2-inch gauze roll
3-by-3-inch gauze pads

Nail clippers
Q-tips

Quik-stop
Scissors

Snakebite kit (in areas where needed)
Tape

Three-way antibiotic ointment
Vaseline

Vet wrap
Wound cleaner

Dog-to-Human Age Comparison Chart

DOG YEARS	HUMAN YEARS
1	15
2	24
3	28
4	32
5	36
6	40
7	44
8	48
9	52
10	56
11	60
12	64
13	68
14	72
15	76
16	80

Based on: Delbert G. Carlson and James M. Giffon, Dog Owner's Home Veterinary Handbook *(New York: Howell Book House, 1987), p. 356.*

APPENDIX A

*Puppy Vet Schedule**

AGE AT TREATMENT	TREATMENT
Two to three days	Dew claws removed
Four weeks	Worming
Six weeks	Worming First DHPPC shots
Nine weeks	Second DHPPC booster Bordetella Weight Stool check
Twelve weeks	Third DHLPPC booster First Lyme disease shot Weight
Sixteen weeks	Fourth DHLPPC booster Second Lyme disease shot Rabies shot Weight Start heartworm program
Yearly	DHLPPC Booster Lyme disease booster Bordetella Weight
Every two or three years**	Rabies shot

**Alternatives to this vaccination schedule should be discussed with your vet.*
***Check your state's regulation on the frequency of rabies shots.*

My Tuck, AyA, and grouse after a successful hunt.

up of your family. The family is pleased and proud because it does so. Untrained dogs lead lives that are frustrating to both them and their owners.

With a lifetime of experience in athletics and dogs, no moment inspires me more than the first time a young pup locks on scent point, quivering in anticipation. It is no accident! Good breeding and good handling produce outstanding performers. With both of these and plenty of birds, your pup can become a very satisfactory companion gun dog.

CONCLUSION

Reaping the Benefits

I t's important to start with a pup that has gun-dog breeding, one that will point, retrieve, and even back naturally, and do it at a comfortable range and pace. Choosing a type and breed that suit your use and personality will ensure the greatest success. The big four breeds in pointing-dog circles—English setters, pointers, German shorthairs, and brittanies—are popular for a reason: They have consistently produced the most top performers. Gun dogs should be bred for hunting attitude, conformation, and temperament. A bloodline that consistently possesses all of these characteristics is admirable. All breeds have good individuals, but if you choose to go with a rare breed, do your research carefully. Also research the breeder carefully and be sure he or she is breeding dogs for the type of hunting you do. Do not expect a dog with field-trial or show breeding to make a good gun dog. Gun dogs are bred for a specific purpose. Championships in a pedigree may be as much a problem as a blessing; it depends on what type of championships they are. I breed and hunt dual-type English setters because they fit my style of hunting and personality. Your choice should do the same for you.

Once you have chosen the correct pup, proper care and handling will help develop a healthy, happy gun dog and a rewarding relationship. Spend time with your pup, and start working with it right away. The first year in a pup's life is equivalent to fifteen in a person's. Imagine a fifteen-year-old with no socialization or education. Become a team, and appreciate your pup for what it brings to the partnership. A true companion gun dog is as priceless as a field-trial or show dog.

Once your dog has been properly trained, it can lead a relaxing, rewarding life without fear of constant harassment. It knows what is expected of it, and by doing so, it fulfills its role in the social group made

108

dog clearly understands what is expected of it, so it relaxes and becomes a more efficient hunter. Everyone enjoys the hunting experience more fully. My clients often comment on how much more relaxed their dogs are once they have been collar-broken. This occurs both because the dog understands its job more clearly and because the handler is more calm and confident also. I also teach most clients' dogs the quartering or "this way" command with preconditioning and use of an e-collar. The technique is similar to that for the "come" command.

Remote trainers work when properly applied, and amazingly to the novice, they are more humane than many traditional training methods. I do not train my own dogs with an e-collar, however, and I do not introduce it in the field. In fact, if you do use one with proper technique, you will have to use it very little in the field. You must still train the dog in the traditional manner as outlined in this text. Once the dog knows what is expected of it but is not responding correctly, you can use the e-collar to finish its training, gaining absolute control. The dog is introduced to the collar in a controlled environment in a manner that guarantees success. My e-collar program uses two yard sessions followed by two field sessions, with a progressive technique to engrain coming and quartering to the whistle. After this is done, the dog can be handled in the field almost flawlessly.

Once the dog is accustomed to the collar for handling, you can use it to finish other aspects of training. The level of stimulation needed will vary with every dog. It should only be high enough to get the job done. You are not out to cause pain, just to tap the dog on the shoulder to get its attention. The higher levels are for serious misbehavior, such as deer chasing. Improper use of the collar, either too much or too frequent stimulation, will make it ineffective and perhaps ruin your dog.

The ultimate goal of using an e-collar is to no longer need it. This can be accomplished by appropriate preconditioning in the yard and consistent application in the field for proper whistle response. Correctly used, the collar will become unnecessary once the collar- to-whistle association has been so engrained in the dog's mind that it will correctly respond to the whistle alone.

I will not go into detail on specific applications for e-collars. You need to seek professional help in choosing the correct e-collar for your situation and in proper use of it.